Retirement Facilities

RETIREMENT FACILITIES

PLANNING, DESIGN, AND MARKETING

**RAYMOND J. GOODMAN, JR., PH.D.
AND DOUGLAS G. SMITH, A.S.I.D.**

WHITNEY LIBRARY OF DESIGN

An imprint of Watson-Guptill
Publications/New York

TO MY WIFE, HELEN
—RJG

TO MY GRANDMOTHER, ELVA ROUSELL,
WHO, IN SPITE OF HER MEAGER CIRCUMSTANCES,
TAUGHT ME THAT ALL HUMAN BEINGS, INCLUDING THE
ELDERLY, DESERVE A TRUE MEASURE OF DIGNITY
—DGS

Editor: Paul Lukas
Designer: Areta Buk
Senior Editor: Roberto De Alba
Production Manager: Ellen Greene

Copyright © 1992 by *Restaurant/Hotel Design International*

First published in 1992 by Whitney Library of Design,
an imprint of Watson-Guptill Publications,
a division of BPI Communications, Inc.,
1515 Broadway, New York, NY 10036

Library of Congress Cataloging-in-Publication Data

Goodman, Raymond J.
    Retirement facilities : planning, design, and marketing / Raymond
J. Goodman, Jr., Douglas G. Smith.
        p.   cm.
    ISBN 0-8230-4551-X
    1. Old age homes—United States—Planning.   2. Retirement
communities—United States—Planning.   3. Life care communities—
United States—Planning.   4. Aged—United States—Dwellings—
Planning.   5. Aged—United States—Dwellings—Marketing.
I. Smith, Douglas G., 1952–   . II. Title.
HV1454.2.U6G66   1992
362.1′6′068—dc20   91-34239
                                                                    CIP

Manufactured in Singapore

First printing, 1992

1 2 3 4 5 6 7 8 9 / 98 97 96 95 94 93 92

ACKNOWLEDGMENTS

First and foremost, we wish to acknowledge M. J. Madigan, editor and publisher of *Restaurant/Hotel Design International* magazine, who saw the opportunity and the need for a book on retirement center design. Without M. J.'s vision, this book would not have been published.

Second, we wish to thank the designers, architects, and photographers whose creative work we reproduced, and who allowed us to do so.

There were many other people who helped with research, content, editing, administration, and other tasks too numerous to detail. We list them randomly, without regard to either their level of contribution or alphabetization: David Wolfe, Mary Malone, Cornelia Guest, Andrew Seibert, Bob Eramian, Barbara Kleger, H. B. "Skip" Kedney, Katrinka Sloan, Janice Gray, Jim Moore, Jim Sherman, Evelyn Howard, Frank Rees, Carl Irwin, Chuck Griffin, David Schless, Frank Romano, Chris Olney, Arlene Thompson, Robert MacKenzie, Marjorie Gove, Neil Vroman, Arnold Linsky, Fred Kaen, Ann Badger, Joe Durocher, Regina Baraban, Joe Danehy, Susan Brecht, Richard Jaffe, Mel Gamzon, Bruce Mondschain, Penny Pritzker, the University of New Hampshire Interdisciplinary Committee on Aging, George Bradish, Terry Toomey, Ralph Bellande, Jeff Olsen, Jeff Sohl, Chris Mason, Leo Baldwin, Paul Lukas, Roberto De Alba, Areta Buk, Ellen Greene, William Weathersby, Jr., Todd Underwood, Sinthy Kounlasa, George Genung, Cheryl Eyre, Ben Pearce, Becky Sperry, Mary Malone, Michelle Hawkins, Karl Pillemer, and the students in the first Business and Aging class at the Whittemore School of Business at the University of New Hampshire.

CONTENTS

FOREWORD

As Raymond Goodman and Doug Smith's book goes to press, the U.S. retirement housing industry is in a state of great distress. It is an industry still in search of a modus operandi for success.

In the past seven or eight years, during which the for-profit sector has attempted to make major inroads in a field formerly dominated by nonprofit organizations, little progress has been made in creating living environments into which most oldsters *want* to move. Award-winning designs, competitive pricing, and superb marketing techniques have characterized many of the more than six hundred projects that have nonetheless been taken back by lenders and mortgage guarantors in the last several years.

As new retirement communities continue to come on line with disappointing results for their sponsors, design features and marketing techniques continue to be tinkered with in the elusive quest for the answers. But the sources of widespread failure in the industry are less tangible than intangible.

Barry Bukoff, quoted in this book, places his finger squarely on the root of the problems when he says that designers must "[let] go of their egocentric needs to have the 'right' solution, and [allow] free and equal exchange of ideas." Indeed, the difficulties being experienced in the retirement housing industry do not so much derive from the consumer side as from the provider side. As Bukoff suggests, the source of problems leading to failed design is the human ego. Not just the egos of design professionals—the insistence of other participants in the design, marketing, and operating domains to impose their own ego-borne imprints on the project conspires against the achievement of consumer-oriented consensus decisions, without which the consumer will only reluctantly respond.

It is not easy to follow Bukoff's recipe for better design. American society, by nature a highly competitive culture, penalizes those who proffer thought with considered diffidence and, in turn, rewards those with clever aggressiveness.

The American propensity for expression of individualism at the expense of social connectedness is a mixed blessing—the American ethos of the individual has certainly produced technological wonders, and, until recently, an unprecedented standard of living, but at the price of humanistic values.

By depressing the ego factor in design, marketing, and operational processes, the consumer ascends to a higher level of influence in the evolution of a retirement community. This, in turn, creates a social connectedness between provider and consumer that minimizes the gap between project decisions and consumer needs and expectations. Dr. Goodman and Mr. Smith are issuing a call for a return to this social connectedness through the injection of humanistic values into senior living environments, a call that is clearly evident in the comprehensive list of topics covered in this volume. *Retirement Facilities* contains all the basic elements for a revolutionary approach to the design, marketing, and, ultimately, the operation of full-service senior housing. Anything less leaves some of the most important needs of the older housing consumer unattended, with the result that most elderly consumers will remain uninterested. I have spoken with countless seniors about full-service housing, and only the slimmest percentage of them have a positive view of life in a retirement community. I can only conclude that we have been offering the equivalent of ice cubes to Eskimos: What we offer, they already have; what they want, we don't have.

Dr. Goodman and Mr. Smith lay out the recipe for success in retirement housing, but any recipe requires the hands and minds of competent chefs if the finished product is to achieve the potential of its ingredients. All the team members of a new project should be required to read this book, then to participate in an in-depth discussion of its contents and meanings before the first pencil stroke is made on paper.

David B. Wolfe
August, 1991

PREFACE

Although retirement homes have existed for quite some time, having grown out of church-supported residences for displaced seniors, the retirement industry as we know it today is only about 10 years old. The recent rapid entry of the private sector and hotel management operating companies into retirement center management is a clear signal that older adults will be offered impressive yet functional design and exquisite service in their residential settings. But the rush of new developers to capitalize on the growth and wealth of today's elderly and to create a new senior life-style will yield many products that, while beautiful, are neither functional nor flexible. These will be difficult to sell to the sophisticated senior consumer.

A number of senior marketing specialists caution both residential developers and consumer product companies not to consider all seniors as a homogeneous market. Careful analysis must be conducted to pinpoint the specific needs of the target market and to differentiate clearly age and other demographics, psychographic profiles, geographic preferences, and other important distinctions. It is also important to keep in mind that retirement center design differs from nursing home design because most of the retirement facility residents are demand-driven rather than need-driven—they *choose* to live in the environment. Moreover, retirement center design differs significantly from hotel design because residents live in the space permanently and do not check out after a two-, three-, or four-day stay. Indeed, the degree of complexity in planning and designing a retirement center is immense. The designs we see today will continue to change to meet the needs of those middle-aged adults who will soon be looking for retirement in a congregate setting.

M. J. Madigan, editor and publisher of *Restaurant/Hotel Design International*, recognized the need of functional, exquisite design to meet the very specific seniors markets, as well as the need for complementary design features to enhance service delivery. She invited us to write this book to address the planning, design, and marketing of retirement centers for center directors and for architects, designers, planners, and developers wishing to work in this field. In addition, we found ourselves addressing the needs of university students studying architecture and design, social work, gerontology, psychology, sociology, and business and hotel administration with an interest in serving the wide-ranging needs of older adults.

The collaboration of a retirement center design specialist and a university professor to research and develop this text, each from his own perspective, was creative and risky. While the creative description can only be assessed after the text has been reviewed, used, and reviewed again, we feel the endeavor has already yielded a tangible return, even if only in terms of demonstrating to us and, we hope, to others just how much there is to consider in this challenging area. This book only begins to introduce a new thought process to addressing seniors' needs, one that we hope will result in a design product to satisfy the market.

THE EFFECTS OF AGING ON DESIGN

As this is an introductory book designed for individuals who are not familiar with retirement living, senior citizens, aging, and all their related topics, this discussion on aging is, by necessity, a primer—an introduction to aging and its impact on the design of retirement housing for seniors. The purpose here is to introduce the reader to the market segments and individuals for whom residential community products are being designed.

There are definite physical changes that occur as we age. Although we begin aging as soon as we are born, the effects of what the general public defines as aging are manifested shortly after 40 years of age.

To be sure, when we say that we are designing for an aging population, we should think of designing for physical and mental impairments, rather than designing for age alone. Age increases our susceptibility to certain impairments, but it does not necessarily bring on these impairments. Indeed, many people considered to be senior citizens may have fewer impairments than individuals who are younger. Nonetheless, the biological factors of aging should be considerations for design and management, since we are designing for the *average* person, rather than for an individual person. In general, aging decreases the ability of the body to function properly and efficiently, making it more difficult for the body to maintain homeostasis (stable chemical and physical states).

Each of our special senses requires contrasts: brightness/dimness, hot/cold, sweet/sour/bitter, rough/smooth, loud/soft, and so on. We learn to appreciate or assign value to the depth of our experiences in terms of these contrasts, and our sense of enjoyment is heightened by our previous experiences with discomfort. Conversely, discomfort is deepened by our memories of enjoyment. The human mind requires this constant analysis of relative experiences. As we age, the reality of our frailties becomes more apparent. Factors contributing to this include genetics, nutrition, exercise, sleep patterns, social/emotional outlook (including spiritual beliefs), preventive health maintenance, exposure to health risks, and so forth.

Older adults are often unable to detect as much sensory information from their environments as younger people. First, let us examine the five senses as we begin to explore the biological factors that occur during the aging process.

SIGHT

Far-sightedness is a common, age-related, progressive dysfunction caused by the lens of the eye growing increasingly inflexible. As people age, they need more light in order to see at the same level they did when they were younger. The lens of the eye becomes more opaque, thickens, hardens, and becomes yellow. The eyes cannot adjust as rapidly to changes in illumination levels. While a higher degree of illumination is required, glare becomes a more acute problem. Bright, sparkling lights present special problems for seniors (Spence 1988): "As new cells develop on the surface of the lens and the old fibers are compressed, the . . . cells . . . form very small opaque regions, . . .

CARRINGTON POINTE, FRESNO, CALIFORNIA

ABOVE: The thick stucco walls and tile roof of the Spanish Colonial Carrington Pointe community building hold up well to the temperature extremes of the region and require little upkeep. (Architecture: The Taylor Group; interiors: Struble Chambers Design Associates; photo: Scot Zimmerman.)

SURREY PLACE, CHESTERFIELD, MISSOURI

The stained-glass window above the chapel entry was designed by Lea von Kaenel "to be inspirational rather than religious." (Architecture: The Wischmeyer Architects; interiors: LVK Associates; chairs: Kimball; carpet: Shaw Commercial Carpet; photo: Alise O'Brien.)

CARLETON-WILLARD VILLAGE, BEDFORD, MASSACHUSETTS

ABOVE: New England fieldstone is used for the fireplace in the billiard room, and burnt-orange walls enhance the warm ambiance. (Architecture: TRO/The Ritchie Organization; interiors: Adner/Woodman Design; wing chairs: Shelby Williams with Robert Allen fabric; cocktail table: Shelby Williams; drapery fabric: Coral of Chicago; blinds: Verosol; lamps: Deena Lighting; photo: Robert Mikrut.)

and small, bright light sources may produce so many reflections that they interfere with vision." When color and light values are the same (as on stairs and floors), it becomes difficult to know where the surfaces start or end. Depth perception and peripheral vision are moderately impaired, and accentuating contrasts on walls or doors can reduce the effects of these impairments. Tunnel vision can be minimized by doglegging or offsetting long hallways and ensuring that outside windows are not designed at the ends of hallways, thereby producing a dark hallway end with a bright light.

Most older adults experience other types of vision disorders. The yellowing of the cornea, lens problems, retinal disorders, myopia, glare problems, clouding of the vitriolic fluid, decreased peripheral vision, and so forth all increase with age. These conditions cause decreased perception of light and color, and recovery time from glare takes longer. Visual patterns also become less distinct, due to reduced abilities to focus and adjust to contrasts.

As the eye's lens becomes yellowed and less transparent with age, certain colors and color intensities are not as

discernible—lavender may appear muddy, purple may seem brown, and blues, greens, and violets may become particularly problematic. It is much easier for older people to see yellows, oranges, and reds, yet these colors can become too intense. Darker and bolder colors need to be used if contrasts are designed for functional as well as for aesthetic purposes, but this too can be overdone. Door frames, light switches, exposed pipes, and other details should be visually prominent to facilitate efficiency and safety as older people move from room to room.

SURREY PLACE, CHESTERFIELD, MISSOURI

TOP LEFT: The residential-care lobby has an octagonal shape and vaulted ceiling. (Architecture: The Wischmeyer Architects; interiors: LVK Associates; chairs, tables: Thonet; window treatment, lamps: American of Martinsville; carpet: Harbinger; upholstery: Thonet, Atlanta Architectural Textiles; photo: Alise O'Brien.)

VILLAGE ON THE GREEN, LONGWOOD, FLORIDA

BOTTOM LEFT: This retirement center surrounds a golf course, with the dining room oriented to provide a view of the course. (Interiors: Donald J. Stanzione Associates; tables: Johnson Industries; dining chairs: Shelby Williams; fabric: Arc-Com; carpet: Couristan; columns, planters: custom designed by DJSA, manufactured by R-Cotta; photo: Dan Forer.)

CLASSIC RESIDENCE BY HYATT, TEANECK, NEW JERSEY

RIGHT: Ron Kollar of Hyatt describes the Wintergarden as the facility's "main event," where residents prefer to congregate. The French-influenced retirement complex has a very residential quality and is not intended as a cutting-edge design statement. (Architecture: Fusco, Shaffer & Pappas, Inc.; interiors: Culpepper, McAuliffe and Meaders, Inc.; carpet: Trafford Park Carpets; seating: Custom Craft, Hospitality Furniture Company; fabric: Kirk Brummel, Maharam, Unika Vaev; tables: Murray's Iron Works, Confab; millwork: Confab; photo: Gabriel Benzur.)

WESTLAKE VILLAGE,
WESTLAKE, OHIO

Fanciful millwork, an intricately
patterned tile floor, and ceiling
fans are among the ingredients
used here to recall a small-town
ice cream parlor. (Architecture:
Shepard, Legan, Aldrian, Ltd.;
interiors: Norman Harvey
Associates, Inc./Jean-Lee Design,
Inc.; armchairs: Shelby Williams
with Cohana Riverdale fabric;
tables: Falcon; floor tile: American
Olean; lighting: Illuminating
Experience; glassware: Libbey;
fans: Casa Blanca; wallcovering:
Collins & Aikman; photo: Robert
W. Shimer/Hedrich Blessing.)

THE SEASONS KENWOOD, CINCINNATI, OHIO

LEFT: In the dining room,
decorative window treatments
help cut the glare while allowing
a view of the nearby parklike
preserve. Downlights and
chandeliers offer relatively high,
uniform illumination, which is
particularly helpful for elderly
residents. (Architecture:
PDT + Co.; interiors: Lynn Wilson
Associates, Inc.; carpet: Durkan
Patterned Carpet; closed-back
chair: Bibi Contract Industries with
Kravet fabric; fiddle-back chair:
Bibi Contract Industries with
Stroheim & Romann fabric; dining
tables: Chairmasters; drapery
fabric: Brunschwig & Fils;
sconces, chandeliers: Georgian
Art Lighting; wallcovering: Kinney
Contract Wallcovering; photo:
Eric Hecktor.)

Although the retina of an 80-year-old perceives one-sixth the light of a 25-year-old's, this does not immediately signify a need for increased general light levels in a retirement facility. Usually, a better use of the existing light source will solve the problem. This involves light placement and degrees of reflectance, absorption, and diffusion. When planning for these variables, keep in mind that lighting can readily affect mood and can tease our perceptions toward enjoyment or unpleasantness in a given setting. Lighting placement can heighten or lower our line of vision, and can make us perceive closeness or distance and spaciousness or intimacy at a glance. Light can help us gain orientation, avoid danger, and perceive textural richness or plainness. Light reflectance helps us perceive color, which in turn can animate or calm us.

How does this translate into specific design solutions for the older adult? Lighting solutions should focus upon the generalized needs of the particular population that will be using a given facility. Usually, we design for a median of acuity needs. When addressing the issue of corridors, for example, some differences exist between criteria for a congregate housing facility and for a skilled nursing facility. The key factor is the resident's visual perception ability.

Lighting in seniors environments should be of medium brightness, except in task-specific areas. For example, washing walls with indirect light is an effective method of lighting the corridors without producing "hot spots." A bare light bulb should never be exposed to view without shading. Bare windows should be covered with a window covering that diffuses the incoming light, to avoid contrast and glare problems.

As we age, our ability to adjust quickly from light to dark contrasts is slower. In fact, this can cause disorientation and dizziness, especially when the eye and brain are called upon to process a repetitive series of high and low lighting extremes in rapid succession. An example of this would be using pools of direct light on a floor or wall, spaced evenly down a corridor, creating an effect of successive light and dark pools running the length of the corridor—this requires too much visual and mental adjustment. Downlighting also causes deep shadowing, and is inappropriate for reading and most general tasks. It is effective for lighting *objects*, not people.

LIGHTING LEVELS

ABOVE: The top two images show the effects of poor lighting—high contrast between lighted surfaces and surrounding areas, creating visual "hot spots," which are particularly disorienting to the elderly. The lower image, with a brighter, more consistent level of illumination, is better suited to older residents. (Generated on LumenMicro software.)

HEATHERWOOD AT KINGS WAY, YARMOUTH, MASSACHUSETTS

FACING PAGE: The elegant lobby establishes Heatherwood's color scheme—a sophisticated version of a traditional colonial palette. (Architecture: Woo & Williams and Hammer, Kiefer & Todd; interiors, art, accessories: Design 1 Interiors; lamps: Stiffel; console, table: Council Companies; carpet: Milliken; window treatments: Designer Workroom Services with Stroheim & Romann fabric; upholstery: Unique Designs; photo: Cymie Payne.)

Indirect troffer or valance lighting is particularly useful for offering an even illumination to wall and floor surfaces. While it is preferable to light wall surfaces brightly, it is not necessary to light flooring surfaces directly. Contrast between wall and floor surfaces should be considered.

As we age, there is a natural tendency to interpret a change in flooring color as a change in flooring height or level. This same depth-perception principle holds true for walls. Extreme contrasts in pattern and value should therefore be avoided throughout floors and walls. Repetitive patterns that appear to move or vibrate will often cause disorientation. In one skilled nursing facility's individual resident rooms, the floor tiles were laid out in what was perceived as a "chic," 12-by-12-inch (30.5-by-30.5-cm) black-and-white checkerboard pattern. Many residents remained in the corners of their rooms or refused to get out of bed, simply because they could not negotiate the complexity of the flooring pattern. The white tiles were seen as stepping stones leading over a dark abyss, making exiting their rooms a psychologically frightening experience.

This same principle can be used to advantage, however, when we wish to warn someone that there is a change in height or depth, such as stairs, busy intersections, key orientation points, countertop edges, or other hazards.

COLOR. Further discussion of the use of color should be mentioned here. The gradual age-related yellowing of the cornea creates the same effect as yellow-tinted glasses. As professionals make color decisions for elderly environments, it is helpful to don yellow glasses to simulate this effect. Many colors literally disappear; other colors with no yellow component, such as lavender, purple, blues, reds, magenta, some browns, and grays, are difficult to perceive. Colors that are at least partially yellow and easily perceived are primary yellow, peach, coral, clay, orange, some pinks, greens, aquas, and some browns. Interestingly, because of their warm tint, most of these yellow-related hues, including aqua, are perceived as "uppers," or mood-elevating. It is not by coincidence that these colors or their derivatives are used in medical environments, where convalescing and recovery are aided by the colors' encouragement of positive, cheerful emotions. Indeed, many designers feel there is a connection between our regenerative and immune systems and our emotional responses.

Many experts claim that stronger colors can, and should, be used for the seniors market. Experience shows that this concept is somewhat overstated, however. Although a strong accent color may be used periodically for punctuation in key areas, pure, primary colors are generally too strong to be useful in large doses, especially for daily exposure.

The color quality of lighting is important in determining the colors we perceive. A cool or blue light source, such as cool fluorescent tube lighting, can cancel out the warmth of certain colors. Conversely, the warm or orange light rendered by incandescent lamps can cancel out the effect of an otherwise well-placed cool color. A trained color professional can assist the designer and the development team in creating the proper luminosity and effect desired in a space. Indeed, the possibilities are vast (Brown 1989, 106):

Research on the effects of brightness patterns began in the 1970's when the late architect John Flynn at Kent State University found that the visible contrasts created by laying light against darkness govern several different human responses. He identified attention, orientation, movement, mood, and our sense of spaciousness.

By attention, he meant that when we walk into a room, we look at the surface that is most brightly lighted as though we expect something to happen there. By orientation, he observed that we move toward light. If we walk into a dim foyer but we see a brighter room down the hall, we gravitate to the brighter room.

With these responses to light, designers have a powerful tool. We can control the movement of people through space.

The pattern of brightness in a room affects almost all of these cues. For instance, in trying to make a room seem smaller or more intimate, we could falsify the size of an object. If we put a white vase against a darker background and light it with a small, intense beam of light, the lighted white object will "grow," therefore altering the proportions of the room and making it appear smaller.

The old bromide that warm colors advance and cool colors recede has been debunked by science . . . Whether a surface is advancing or receding is a result of brightness contrasts or the contrast between light and dark. If we light a room evenly and paint an end wall a darker hue of the color of the two side walls but don't light it, the end wall will seem farther away.

Lighting affects the elevation cue as well. If some visual object is higher in a space than you expect it to be, it seems farther away.

BROOKHAVEN AT LEXINGTON, LEXINGTON, MASSACHUSETTS

Dramatically swagged draperies frame views through the expansive windows in the club room. (Architecture: Russel Gibson von Dohlen; interiors: Arthur Shuster, Inc.; draperies: Schumacher, Fairmont Corp., Scalamandre; lounge chairs: Statesville Chair with Duralee fabric; game chairs: Drexzel Heritage with Robert Allen fabric; casegoods: Drexel Heritage; carpet: Charleston Carpets; wallcovering: Rubin Design Studios; photo: A. F. Payne Photographic.)

WESTLAKE VILLAGE, WESTLAKE, OHIO

In the dining room, two sets of French doors open to an outdoor patio, while others provide access to other parts of the community center. (Architecture: Shepard, Legan, Aldrian, Ltd.; interiors: Horman Harvey Associates, Inc./Jean-Lee Design, Inc.; chairs: Shelby Williams with Waverly fabric; banquettes: Shelby Williams; tables: Falcon; carpet: Harbinger; floral arrangements: Ann Cole Designs; window treatments: Ideal Drapery; wallcovering: Sunwall; lighting: Forecast; border inside cowed ceiling: Arystyl Cove Molding; glassware: Cardinal; flatware: Oneida; napery: Quip Linen; china: Syracuse China; photo: Robert. W. Shimer/Hedrich Blessing.)

BROOKHAVEN AT LEXINGTON, LEXINGTON, MASSACHUSETTS

The café offers an informal, gardenlike spot to enjoy light snacks throughout the day. (Architecture: Russel Gibson von Dohlen; interiors: Arthur Shuster, Inc.; wallcovering: Warner Company; chairs, tables: Drexel Heritage with Warner Company fabric; flooring: International Tile and Supply; window Shutters: Pinecrest; photo: A. F. Payne Photographic.)

THE HEARTWOOD, TACOMA, WASHINGTON

The light-filled solarium offers a pleasant, attractive setting for residents. (Architecture: Merritt & Pardini; interiors: Hendrix Interiors; carpet: Atlas; wood floor: Permagrain Products; area rugs: Pande Cameron; window treatments: Verosol Pleated Shades; chairs: Lowenstein/Oggo with fabrics by Robert Allen Fabrics and vinyl by Wolf Gordon; tables and bases: Spectrum Furniture Co.; photo: Mark Rickets Photography.)

CARRRINGTON POINTE, FRESNO, CALIFORNIA

RIGHT: An oversize mural in the community living room picks up the color scheme of green, coral, and peach. The two-sided fireplace faces both the living room and the lounge. Skylights and clerestory windows brighten the space without contributing glare. (Architecture: The Taylor Group; interiors: Struble Chambers Design Associates; mural: Cathie Milner; tile: American Olean; fireplace molding: Machado; tables: Link-Taylor, Dixie Mfg.; seating: Rainbow Upholstery, Sitting Pretty; fabrics: Jack Lenor Larsen, Robert Allen; photo: Scot Zimmerman.)

CARRRINGTON POINTE, FRESNO, CALIFORNIA

ABOVE: A garden theme in the dining room is orchestrated through whimsical greenhouse murals, a hutch full of plants and colorful crockery, and floral chintz upholstery on reproduction country French chairs. The firm chairs have armrests to assist elderly residents in rising. Wall sconces provide an ambient light without creating glare. (Architecture: The Taylor Group;

interiors: Struble Chambers Design Associates; mural: Cathie Milner; border: Kinney Brothers; hutch: Drexel Heritage; chairs: L & B with Robert Allen fabric; photo: Scot Zimmerman.)

RIGHT: The library is a popular gathering spot for afternoon tea or a game of cards. Oak bookshelves are lined with books collected by the residents, and

chintz draperies and upholstery brighten the cozy room. The cost-conscious project was completed with a construction budget of $46 per square foot, with furnishings running only $1.19 per square foot. (Architecture: The Taylor Group; interiors: Struble Chambers Design Associates; seating: Rainbow Upholstery with Robert Allen fabric; tables: Link-Taylor; photo: Scot Zimmerman.)

For example, when we run a dark-colored carpet up the baseboard of a wall that is painted a much lighter color, by lighting some other feature in the room we can distract the eye. When the wall with the falsified baseboard technique is seen from a distance, the brain registers that all of the dark area is the floor and all of the light area is the wall. Because the wall seems smaller and higher than it actually is, it must be farther away and, therefore, the room must be larger.

HEARING

In addition to sight, one of the first senses to be affected by age is hearing, and this begins to occur by the age of 40. High-frequency pitches are the first to become less audible or distinguishable; while there is also a reduced sensitivity to lower-frequency pitches, this loss is not severe. The ability to understand normal conversation is usually not disturbed at first, but may diminish, especially when combined with background noise, which can then obstruct comprehension.

Acoustics, therefore, must be designed to minimize background noise. Most elderly people lose their ability to perceive the depth, quality, and subtleties of sound. If acoustics in a large public area are not designed specifically for the elderly, older people may find it difficult or impossible to differentiate background noises from the voice of someone who is talking to them only a few feet away.

Each of our human senses requires contrast to learn discernment, and hearing is no different. This is why we must help those with decreased hearing acuities to optimize their daily experience through better acoustic solutions. Acoustics can be significantly shaped and controlled by architectural detailing. Applied absorptive finish materials can also help areas where sound reverberation is problematic. Areas of particular concern are large, cavernous spaces, such as dining rooms, auditoriums, nursing coves, lobbies, enclosed swimming pools, exercise rooms, therapy rooms and bathing

LA POSADA AT PARK CENTRE, GREEN VALLEY, ARIZONA

ABOVE: The building's cruciform layout allows nurses to view all corridors from a desk at the central axis. The theme of the congregate space is carried to the skilled nursing facility—the U-shaped desk is inviting and approachable, like the concierge desk in the congregate living facility, and the sprightly colored, flame-proofed banners are similar to those seen in the dining rooms of the congregate building. (Architecture: Englebrecht and Griffin; interiors: Life Designs; banners: DesignTex; custom carpet: Durkan Patterned Carpets; vinyl wallcovering: Sinclair; seating: Harter; photo: Ed Rosenberger.)

RIGHT: Residents have two meals per day in the dining room. Banners, changed seasonally to keep the look fresh, add color and absorb sound, while chairs have firm and shallow seats and sturdy arms. The building was oriented so that the dining room has a spectacular view of the desert and the Santa Rita Mountains. (Architecture: Englebrecht and Griffin; interiors: Life Designs; dining chairs: Shelby Williams with Westgate fabric; table bases: CHF; ceiling banners: Decorator's Walk; stemware: Libbey; china: Hall China; flatware: World Tableware International; lighting: Capri; etched glass: Valley Glass; carpet: Durkan Patterned Carpet; photo: Michael Schoenfeld.)

rooms. Architecturally, the more a space is broken up with variations of surface planes and depths of surface textures, the better it will be acoustically.

The principle of *sound absorption* is valid in areas where an appropriate amount of soft-surfaced or sound-absorbing material can be used; ceiling banners, sound panels/baffles, acoustical ceiling tile, carpeting, drapery, plantings, and any other soft surfaces added to the room are examples of sound-absorption design features. Professionals should not, however, depend upon movable room furnishings to solve acoustical problems, since such furnishings are as easily removed from their acoustically

strategic spaces in later years as they were initially moved there. Health codes should always be considered when developing a solution, particularly in wet or steamy areas, such as pool areas or bathing rooms, or in foodservice areas, where sanitation must always be an over-riding consideration.

Unlike visual perception, which usually gives us immediate recognition of comfort or discomfort, acoustic or auditory perception generally requires more time for discernment. It is interesting how we can leave a place with poor acoustics feeling tired, emotionally sapped, or irritable without completely understanding why we feel that way.

Indeed, certain restaurants intentionally utilize no sound-absorptive materials, in order to facilitate a high customer-turnover rate. Designers of these spaces specify hard-surface tile floors instead of carpeting, and plaster ceilings instead of acoustic materials. To be sure, these environments make normal conversation next to impossible.

TASTE

While some theories suggest that taste-bud sensitivity declines with age, it is also true that changes in the processing of information from the tongue and

THE QUADRANGLE,
HAVERFORD,
PENNSYLVANIA

The enclosed two-story pool pavilion is punctuated with French doors and clerestory windows. Colorful banners enliven the space visually and help reduce sound reverberations.
(Architecture and landscape design: Wallace Roberts & Todd; interiors: Marriott Corporation; photo: Matt Wargo.)

mouth through the nervous system are responsible for a decline in taste, a critical factor in the management and operation of a facility's food and beverage department.

Proper nutrition is a key component in providing an attractive and healthy setting. On the one hand, food has to be more delicately flavored; on the other, it must be appropriately spiced. While salt is a great cure-all for taste purposes, it is generally incompatible with good nutrition and cannot be used at all for those on salt-free diets. A different approach is to consider that food will be enjoyed more if it tastes good. In order to achieve this, the sense of smell must work hand in glove with taste.

SMELL

Of all the senses, smell can evoke the quickest and deepest responses, often without conscious knowledge of its effect. A familiar smell can awaken memories of something experienced many years ago, often with strong emotional impact. As we age, our sense of smell is one of the first senses to become impaired. There is a slight reduction in the overall ability to smell, and stronger differentiations are required in order to make distinctions, especially regarding food. To many aged individuals, food no longer seems appetizing, bathing seems no longer necessary, and housekeeping may not seem as vital. Often, this is not due to lack of mobility or hunger, but because they literally do not sense odors, whether appetizing, inviting, or foul. As we move through our environment, we are virtually "tasting" our way, through smell—the experience can be either neutral, pleasant, or unpleasant. To the aged individual, however, life may seem flat, simply because there is a sameness about all odors (or an absence of them). Imagine the aromas of a roasting turkey, an expensive perfume, or foul sewage; now imagine these smells losing their distinctions.

Currently, there is not a lot that can be done to compensate for this olfactory deficit. In order to heighten the dining experience for the individual senior, food can be presented in a more visually attractive and appetizing manner, but little can be done to enhance food aroma. There are, however, a number of issues that can be addressed in a facility to overcome ongoing stereotypes of the foul odor of the convalescent home: Building systems can be planned to accommodate higher than average levels of air circulation; maintenance systems should be designed to determine if the methods and frequency of maintenance are meeting the true housekeeping needs of the facility and its residents; cleaning solutions and applications should be planned for and reviewed.

Many facilities today are using odor-resistant carpeted floors in areas where this was deemed impossible in years past. This is due to advances in subsurface floor sealants and in liquid-impervious floor-backing materials. (This solution, incidentally, has helped acoustics immensely.) On many wall, counter, cabinet, and flooring surfaces, there are materials impervious to absorption and decay that can be used, including glass, ceramic tile, acrylic grout, plastic laminate, vinyl sheeting, polyester resinous sheeting, decorative sheet metal, stone, and acrylic impregnated wood. All of these contribute to an environment that will maintain an odor-free setting over years of long-term use.

Similar effects are obtainable in other areas: Movable furnishings with a subsurface upholstery shield of liquid-repellent vinyl can now be obtained; many surface coverings may now be vinylized; advances in the visual and tactile detailing of opaque vinyl has now rendered them with the appearance of fabric. Well-conceived design solutions, adequate budget allowances, and a commitment to good routine maintenance can help a facility maintain a reputation for a pleasant, odor-free environment.

TOUCH

The sense of touch helps us heighten the reality of our experiences. Consciously, we use touch to tell us that objects are tangible and real; subconsciously, all human beings intuitively understand the adage, "What I can touch, I can believe in!"

Variance of texture can help us discern whether an object is plain or complicated. Touch can also tell us whether something is hot or cold. Touch can help us legitimize size and detailing of an object. Touch alone (or the lack thereof) can tell us if something or someone is comfortable, painful, familiar, and so forth. Touch can be used as a wayfinding technique, to guide us toward safety or from physical hazards. Just as sight-impaired people of any age tend to rely more heavily on touch, elderly people can do likewise—as acuities of other senses decrease, a method for enhancing life experiences through touch can become more prominent.

Aging brings a reduced sensitivity to both hot and cold. Because reaction time is also slower, water-heating systems need to be calibrated to prevent scalding. Heating, ventilating, and air conditioning systems in buildings designed for older adults must be more sensitive, too. Likewise, heat and high temperatures are cause for more concern, since there is a higher mortality rate from heat prostration among the elderly.

More attention can and should be devoted to the quality of our tactile experience while moving through a space. Is a handrail smooth and comfortable to grasp? Is it secure and warm, or wobbly and cold? Are there art objects and accessories that say "please touch me" to be appreciated? Is attention paid to hardware and plumbing fittings that are comfortable to touch and use? Are coverings and finishes tactually appealing, or are they repelling? Are countertop edgings comfortable to the touch, or are they sharp? Might they tear the thin skin of an elderly person? These questions must be considered by planners designing for seniors.

In addition to the senses, there are other aging-related factors that should be considered when designing and operating a facility for seniors.

BODY STRUCTURE AND COMPOSITION

There is a loss of height during aging, becoming noticeable around 40, and a corresponding muscle deterioration that

reduces the average size of an older person compared to a younger one. While
we gain weight after midlife, we begin
to lose weight at about the middle 50s
for men and the middle 60s for women.
The major design implication here is that
shelf and cabinet heights should be appropriate for the smaller stature of an
older person.

The skin becomes thinner during
aging, making it more susceptible to cutting or tearing. The design must avoid
sharp surfaces and rough wall surfaces
(stucco, for instance).

MEMORY AND MENTAL IMPAIRMENT

Contrary to popular belief, the only
mental impairment that can be *directly* at-
tributed to age is the loss of short-term
memory. Signage and other memory
cues, such as different-colored floor
levels within a multistory structure, aid
in the normal functioning of a resident in
a senior facility. Spatial patterns and
circulation routes must be simple to
avoid confusion. Building products that
send conflicting signals about the

environment (e.g., visually or tactilely contrasting surfaces) should be avoided. Yet, the more "noticeable changes that accompany the reduction of brain mass are those associated with learning new skills. In fact, in older persons there is a greater decline in speed of response and ability to integrate what is observed than there is in verbal ability or memory" (Spence 1988).

EMOTIONAL RESPONSES

Older people almost always find leaving their home environments, family, friends, and usually most of their familiar furniture and material possessions and moving into facilities for the elderly to be a traumatic experience, wrought with emotions. Of course, this is not the only emotional trauma common to the elderly—seniors may experience the loss of spouses, loved ones, and friends, loneliness, the loss of their careers, and illnesses. Unsurprisingly, then, the incidence of depression among the elderly is twice as high as for the general public.

The suicide rate for seniors is the highest of any age group. Alcoholism and substance abuse are also growing problems among the older adult population. For these reasons, special attention must be given to the emotional needs of the residents of all types of senior living centers.

One key reason that older adults reside in group settings is to avoid being alone, so it is important to design sociability into the environment. Amenity areas where people congregate should be situated where residents naturally pass by. For some seniors, mail and meals are the only activities that draw them out of their private living spaces, so mailboxes should be placed in an area where people may socialize if they wish.

Step-down socialization, a term used to describe the process of limited social engagement, suggests design structures formatted to this end. Older people, like everyone else, wish to be alone at certain times. It is important for the design to allow for private space by giving residents the option to gracefully avoid active social involvement, or to merely observe rather than participate directly. It is

beneficial to place smaller social or reading rooms near the larger social gathering points, to let people get off by themselves or with one or two companions without feeling isolated. When planning seating in lounges and dining rooms, it is wise to have seating for one or two, as well as larger tables for groups or tables that can be moved together for even larger groups. Square tables that can be easily increased in size by adding leaves are particularly useful. In dining rooms, a 36-by-36-inch (91-by-91-cm) table module is ideal for this type of flexible grouping. A 24-by-30-inch (61-by-76-cm) table is ideal for accommodating one or two persons.

Overplanning is a common mistake of designers and owners of senior living facilities. By planning and furnishing every square inch of space, designers leave no room for individualization by residents. Many older adults residing in retirement facilities have moved out of much larger spaces and wish to bring antiques, art objects, furniture, and other personal items that they had in their homes and donate them to the facility.

LA POSADA AT PARK CENTRE, GREEN VALLEY, ARIZONA

Knowing that residents will always show up early for mail and meals, the design team created a predining area where the residents can mill about, socialize, and enjoy music. (Architecture: Englebrecht and Griffin; interiors: Life Designs; sofa: Designline with Brunschwig & Fils fabric; upholstered chairs: Shelby Williams, Dependable; custom carpet: Durkan Patterned Carpets; upholstery fabrics: Westgate, Brunschwig & Fils; throw pillow fabric: Carolyn Ray; sandstone coffee table: People-of-the-Forest; Stucco ceiling finish: Ameritone; table lamp: Lamps Plus; photo: Ed Rosenberger.)

WESTLAKE VILLAGE, WESTLAKE, OHIO

Lounges on the main floor of each residential unit provide a spot for individual or group activity. Handrails are disguised as decorative chair rails. (Architecture: Shepard, Legan, Aldrian, Ltd.; interiors: Norman Harvey Associates, Inc./Jean-Lee Design, Inc.; tables: Hekman; chairs: Harden with Lazarus Contract fabric; desk: Dixie; art: Edward Art; wallcovering above chair rail: Metro; wallcovering below chair rail: Genon; photo: Robert W. Shimer/Hedrich Blessing.)

CLASSIC RESIDENCE BY HYATT, TEANECK, NEW JERSEY

By dividing the large space in two, setting off table groupings with partitions, and keeping the ceiling low, the interior design team created a dining room that is elegant and intimate. (Architecture: Fusco, Shaffer & Pappas, Inc.; interiors: Culpepper, McAuliffe and Meaders, Inc.; carpet: Trafford Park Carpets; seating: hospitality Furniture Company; fabric: AAT, J. H. Thorpe; china: Lenox; flatware: Oneida; napery: Artex; glassware: Cardinal; porcelain: Jane Marsden; chandelier: Alger Lighting; photo: Gabriel Benzur.)

This is a strong emotional need for many seniors vacating their primary residences, some of which they occupied for several decades. If overplanning has already taken place, new additions of beautiful pieces to the facility cannot be accommodated. The importance of allowing residents to personalize their new environments, and to endow their new residence with a remnant of what gave their previous homes a sense of place, should not be overlooked. (A word of caution in accepting personal items for public display: Allow for the tactful rejection of objects that would be out of place. This allows an operator to maintain the facility's aesthetic integrity. A facility may have a review board that assesses proposed donations of furnishings or artwork, protecting the center's staff from conflicts and bitter feelings.

Indeed, other provisions must be made for ensuring the safety of residents' publicly displayed personal items from fire, theft, and so forth.

Considerations in social programs and physical structures should address the psychology of need for public and private space. It should allow for the opportunity of gradual or instant communal involvement, as well as for individualistic efforts. There should be areas of individualization and personalization of space, and there should also be visible common areas that residents may develop in a communal effort to give their facility a feeling of "home." This can be achieved through familiarity, a sense of contribution and belonging.

Woven throughout the discussion of emotional needs is the important concept of *choice*, and of giving the older adult

residents personal options in creating personal and public space to promote their independence. Relocation to a retirement facility is generally accompanied by a narrowing of choices in life, and planning should take pains to expand choices by encouraging residents to furnish their living spaces with their own furniture, personal items, paintings and sculpture.

Many development team professionals do not empathize with the seniors who will be experiencing life in the settings that the professionals are creating. This lack of empathy, unfortunately, is found at all levels—developers, owners, operators, managers, health care providers, housekeeping staff, architects, engineers, foodservice managers, construction workers, interior designers, and on and on. Frequently, a designer or

THE FORUM AT
OVERLAND PARK, KANSAS

Light colors were specified for the dining room, to give it an open, airy feeling. (Architecture: National Architectural Services; interiors: I.D.A.; chairs: Shelby Williams with fabric by Waverly, Robert Allen; tables: Shelby Williams; carpet: Shaw Industries, Bentley Carpet Mills; wallcovering: Waverly; draperies: Waverly with fabric by Sherrill Draperies; photo: Tom Sanders/Architectural Fotographics.)

THE QUADRANGLE,
HAVERFORD,
PENNSYLVANIA

An existing manor house provides
the facade for the Quadrangle,
imparting a traditional, collegiate
air to the senior living community.
(Architecture and landscape
design: Wallace Roberts & Todd;
interiors: Marriott Corporation;
photo: Matt Wargo.)

architect designs a space from an intellectual, unemotional point of view, or from an external perspective. Designers need to spend more time considering the concerns of those who will be using the space continuously.

Even as our universities are filling up with senior citizens returning to school to advance their knowledge, many people still believe that old people "think a certain way" or are "rigid" or "live in the past." On the contrary, the majority of seniors today are visionary and ambitious. To be sure, marketers are finding senior consumers' acceptance levels of many new products and services surprising, especially when the products and services are value-driven. The message to planners here is, "Don't underestimate the older adult!" Freshness and innovation *are* welcome in this customarily tradition-steeped industry. To assume that a senior will accept a product, service, or design simply because it is old-fashioned or traditional is erroneous and dangerous. Moreover, most older adults say they feel approximately 15 years younger than their chronological age.

SIGNAGE

As we age, our line of vision is lowered. This is due in part to the deterioration of the spinal discs, as well as loss of muscle control in the neck region. Many older adults are seen with the symptoms of a stooped back or a lowered head. Peripheral vision is diminished, making it more difficult to take in as much without turning the head from side to side. One result of all this is a need to give more advanced warning of hazards. Raised or recessed lettering makes for easier reading as it reduces glare and provides a bolder contrast than flat, printed lettering. Signage, artwork, alarm buttons, elevator call buttons, and so forth should be mounted at lower, more comfortably viewed levels. Consider, for instance, that the average American female over 65 years old is 5 feet, 3 inches (160 cm) tall. Her actual standing height is less as a result of slouch and compression of the fibrous discs between the vertebrae. Her average standing height with a cane or crutch drops to 4 feet, 10 inches (147 cm), and to 3 feet, 10 inches (117 cm) in a wheelchair.

Directional signs are particularly good in assisting in wayfinding, especially if short-term memory loss is encountered. Signage should be simple in message and/or symbology, and should be located in logical areas. Color contrast should be high between the background and text. In facility areas where residents have profound blindness, all signs should have braille messages. In a sense, the facility should be bilingual—visual and tactile.

Several features of a facility can contribute to more effective wayfinding for users. The designer should ask these questions when designing a facility:

1. Have planners considered easy orientation for first-time users?
2. Is there a logical flow between the exterior and interior of the building? Are entryways and key destination points laid out with easy access and visibility in mind?
3. Is there visual access to exterior features that give the user quick reference to overall building orientation (e.g., north, south, east, west) throughout the facility?

4. Are floor levels, wings, departments, and other important regions of the building easily identifiable?
5. Are long runs of corridors kept to a minimum, or broken up with special treatments (e.g., lighting, color, or pattern changes, design detail changes, etc.)? Is egress made easier by direct runs or 90-degree angles, rather than by confusing angles and circuitous detours?
6. Are frequently used services located in easily found areas of the building?
7. Is the overall layout of the building simple to memorize (e.g., T, L, H, or X formations)?
8. Are signage messages presented in short, easily understood phrases? Are messages presented consistently and in a hierarchical priority (e.g., building region, room number, room title)? Is color contrast and value markedly different from text to background in all signage? Is the typeface legible and bold?
9. Is the signage mounted at a comfortable height for all users? Are directories and maps located in prominent locations? Are directories easy to use by lay users? Are informational directories updated on a regular basis?

Our cognitive processes are influenced by current sensory experience interpreted relative to historical experience. It is through this process that we perceive things that are familiar, safe, dangerous, and so on. When numbering and titling rooms, it is important to assign numbers in logical sequences. Egress routes, including handicapped exits, should be identified clearly. Because memory-impaired individuals may find remembering a name or a number to be difficult, sometimes it is appropriate to mount a picture adjacent to a sign. Another important wayfinding feature, especially for the cognitively impaired, is *redundant cueing*, the sending of a message to more than one sensory mode. For example, alarms that emit visual as well as audible signals are helpful for the hearing-impaired. These alarms emit a red flashing signal or a bright strobe light in addition to the typical bell or siren. In the late 1990s, it is likely that codes will

require corridors and exits to utilize a sequential strobe or chaser-type series of egress warning lights, much like those in aircraft cabins, leading residents to marked exits.

Another way to warn people of hazards is by the use of tactile signals, such as vibrating alarm systems. To warn people of busy intersections at corridors or other dangerous areas, a change in flooring texture can be used, not unlike the girded road surfaces that alert drivers of an approaching toll booth. For residents who are not sight-impaired, a change in lighting level and surrounding color of finishes can signal the need for caution.

There are several techniques that can be used to create illusions of warmth and intimacy as well as spaciousness and grandeur. The Japanese create an illusion of space by creating multiple depth layers in framing a view. An individual is beckoned to explore further, passing through or around screening. This technique of peek-through screening creates an illusion of more space. By a false framing of peripheral boundaries, a close view and a small space can actually be made to appear larger and farther away. By focusing the attention in a room on a singular object or feature, such as by intensely lighting the object, the senses can be tricked to enjoy the feeling of more space. For example, one brightly lit focal object and a darkened surrounding background can make a space feel smaller, if the brightly illuminated object is near us. If it is located in the distance, the object will make the room seem larger, due to the sense of distance. Because human beings, like other animals and especially insects, are phototropic (drawn to light), our eyes will always focus on the most brightly illuminated object in a room, whether it is a bare light bulb, a design feature, or an outside view.

The notion of *spaciousness* may seem to be an ill-defined, nebulous subject. There are, however, specific features that give us sensory signals regarding surrounding space. One is our sense of enclosure; another is our perception of the distance from the farthest horizon point; a third is how complex a space appears. Whenever we enter a room, our

subconscious instantly perceives the degree of enclosure. Our eye will usually select the farthest wall, start at the left corner of that wall, and then scan the environment counterclockwise. The mental estimate of this distance gives us our initial perceptions of how large a space is. The perceived spaces between the other three walls and between the floor and ceiling are also important in determining our sense of how large a space is. All of these elements can be made to advance or recede with the skillful use of color and light.

Complexity of a space's background also contributes to how large the space seems. The more intricate or complicated a visual field becomes, through clutter, pattern, and so on, the longer we take to assess the field, and the larger the space will feel. Because bright room patterns can often affect our mood, orientation, how we move through a room, and how it captures our attention, color contrasts of walls and other surfaces give a planner many opportunities to achieve desired effects. A darker color juxtaposed with surrounding lighter colors will make the darker surface appear to recede, creating the illusion of a larger space.

The following elements can, through skillful use, help us create various illusions of space:

1. Sizes of objects and spaces between them
2. Perspective of converging horizon and boundary lines
3. Contrast and brightness of one or more focal objects against their background
4. Clarity of textural details and definitions
5. Height of horizon lines
6. Sparsity or complexity of visual clutter in a space
7. Framing of a perspective and overlapping of intermediate objects

The quality of light rendered by natural daylight is a welcome attraction to our human sensibilities—it literally attracts us. Indeed, natural light is the standard against which we judge the quality of all other types of light. The

FREEDOM PLAZA, SUN CITY, ARIZONA

Pin-dot carpeting in the elevator lobbies camouflages dirt and stains. Niches display pottery, silk plants, and artwork, giving each landing its own character. (Architecture: Freedom Group Inc.; interiors: Merlino Interior Design Associates; signage: SmithCraft Manufacturing; carpet: Durkan Patterned Carpet; wallcovering: Lappin; chairs, pedestal tables: The Chair Factory; table: Lane Furniture Co.; artwork: Leslie Levy Gallery; pottery: Sedona Art Gallery; photo: James Cowlin.)

need for development teams to introduce as much natural light as possible throughout a senior's residential facility cannot be overstressed. This concept is particularly healthful (and, one might add, marketable) when designing individual living units.

STRENGTH AND DEXTERITY

Older people tend to lose strength, and one of the most obvious implications of this is that doors cannot be moved as easily. This, coupled with the loss in dexterity that comes with arthritis, suggests design modifications to facilitate easy access to the building and its components. The design should incorporate door handles and faucet handles that require less-than-normal effort and can be easily manipulated by a senior. Frequently, European-style door handles are used instead of door knobs. Faucet handles are typically the Delta type, with mixers instead of faucet knobs or handles.

EQUILIBRIUM AND BALANCE

The gradual reduction in nervous tissue with age, beginning at 45 and especially noticeable around 70, may affect balance and the coordination of fine movements. Design features that reduce the effect of poor balance include soft landing surfaces and secure footing, both of which are features of carpeting. Flooring should be composed of nonslip surfaces, and should be level, with no protruding seams, cracks, or joints. Patterns that can be perceived to vibrate should be avoided, as they can trigger vertigo, dizziness, and nausea. Wall plugs and telephone plugs can be raised, thereby limiting the need to bend over to reach the outlets. And, of course, support railings are valuable aids for individuals who lack stability when walking.

MOBILITY

Motor skill capacity directly affects options in getting around and in performing simple tasks of daily living. As we age, general motor skills decrease; tasks that were once simple become problematic. Keeping in mind that the purpose in designing facilities for seniors is to maintain the residents' functional independence as human beings, stairs should be replaced by elevators and ramps whenever possible. As always, the goal here should be to assist a senior resident population

LA POSADA AT
PARK CENTRE, GREEN
VALLEY, ARIZONA

The concierge desk is a study in contrasting shapes and materials: Its curved top is mounted on a square base of stucco above brick; the base is trimmed with notched leather belting and whitewashed oak. (Architect: Englebrecht and Griffin; interiors: Life Designs; area rug: Durkan Patterned Carpet; chandelier: Arte de Mexico; glass-top table: Kreiss; photo: Michael Schoenfeld.)

without suggesting that the design is for an impaired or handicapped population. The design features do not need to smack of institutionalism.

There are many subtle and yet effective methods of helping older adults achieve their full potential in mobility and task accomplishment. Simply stated, most older people require more space to get around because of their general instability and the locomotion aids they may need (canes, walkers, and so on). A dining room for a retirement facility is a classic example of this. As a rule, dining rooms are planned on a 15-square-feet-per-person (1.4-square-meters-per-person) basis. But for dining areas for the elderly, 20 to 25 percent more area per person is needed. In the case of wheelchair-bound individuals, this increases to 140 percent more area. Aisle widths between chairs or between furniture and walls should be at least five feet (1.5 meters). Bathrooms, restrooms, and

kitchens are other areas that should be made more space-generous when designing for the elderly.

Gerontology professionals have very divergent viewpoints regarding seating height. It has been found that the elderly can get into and out of chairs more easily if the seat level is higher than normal. But higher seats, while solving one problem, creates another: They are so high that the feet of many of their elderly occupants cannot touch the floor. This is not merely uncomfortable—it can also cause circulation problems. Also, higher seat levels necessitate higher table levels, creating yet another set of problems. All in all, the best solution is normal-level seating—firm, upright, and shallow, with good arm supports to allow the seated individuals to use their arms to pivot or push themselves into an upright position.

Another seating controversy regards whether to use casters on chair legs. On the one hand, the elderly do not have the strength to slide chairs in, out, and around, therefore, necessitating casters; on the other hand, older people often lack the balance they had when they were younger, and chairs with casters can easily roll out from under them. For liability reasons, some seating manufacturers will not sell chairs with casters to retirement facilities. A preferable solution is to install vinyl glides nailed onto the ends of chair legs. These flat little discs allow the chairs to be moved quite easily, and yet give the chairs the stability seniors need. Sled-base chairs also offer a workable solution to better chair-frame stability.

Support elements, such as handrails and grab bars, are both common and necessary in interiors for the elderly.

Unfortunately, the treatment of these elements—where they are placed, how they look, how they feel—is rarely given the attention it deserves. Some interesting design solutions to these issues have been achieved. In one project, a chair rail was run down one side of the corridors, using attractive whitewashed oak wood. On the opposite side of the corridors, a handrail that matched the configuration and color of the chair rail was installed. The handrail merely stuck out farther than the chair rail and was routed out behind, to serve as a hand grasp. The solution was attractive, cost-effective, and functional. It also illustrates the point that the more we work in this field, the more we realize that solutions to the basic functional needs of seniors simply do not have to be ugly,

expensive, or extremely visible. Grab bars offer a similar example: In most facilities, these cold, stainless steel features fairly scream, "This is an institution!" The answer is to install properly blocked brass, wood, or nylon towel bar–type elements that are warmer and much more homelike.

In facilities for the elderly, the types of pulls and levers used on doors and drawers are extremely important. These devices are much easier for older adults to grasp than regular knobs or the various kinds of currently popular finger pulls. They are also much easier to pull because they respond to leverage. A zero- or minimal-resistance hinge is desirable for cabinets; kitchen and bathroom drawers should be able to support an individual's weight.

MEADOWOOD RETIREMENT COMMUNITY, VALLEY FORGE, PENNSYLVANIA

The main lobby, the congregating point for the community, establishes the color palette used throughout the project. Seating here is firm and upright, to accommodate the needs of seniors. (Architecture: CS&D Architects; interiors: Life Designs; planter boxes and tables: Granite Mill; sofas: Doug Duncan; lamps: Frederick Cooper; side chairs: Shelby Williams; carpet: Burtco; sconces: Georgian Art; fabrics: Duralee, Robert Allen, Kravet; photo: Michael Schoenfeld.)

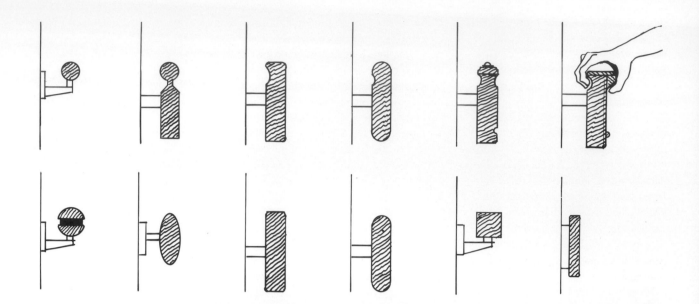

HANDRAIL DETAILS

ABOVE: The top row shows features well suited for retirement facilities, including ideal radius factors and easy graspability for both normal and arthritic residents; the examples on the lower row are not suitable due to size and/or profile.

LA POSADA AT PARK CENTRE, GREEN VALLEY, ARIZONA

The dining room overlooks landscaped gardens. (Architecture: Englebrecht and Griffin; interiors: Life Designs; chairs: Shelby Williams with Westgate Fabrics; carpet: Durkan Patterned Carpet; photo: Michael Schoenfeld.)

In public areas, such as in corridors, chairs should be provided at regular intervals for resting. The trick is to make these appear to be naturally decorative rather than resembling Red Cross stations. Similarly, long corridors are discouraging to the elderly, and therefore should be broken up with doglegs, or other architectural and design elements.

Countertops at information centers, nursing stations, and so forth should be 30 inches (76 cm) high for seated or wheelchair-bound individuals, and 36 inches (91 cm) high for standing individuals. Also, built-in desktops and vanities can be designed to adjust to both normal seating and wheelchair heights.

Public-area furniture, such as in lobbies, should be firm, not too deep, and fairly vertical in pitch. Again, this does *not* mean it has to be ugly—in fact, most styles of upholstered furniture can be adapted upon request by the manufacturer to meet the needs of seniors.

Indeed, more and more manufacturers are responding to the needs of the growing seniors market. Products of this response include appliances with large-type instructions printed on oversized knobs, tubs with collapsible sidewalls for easy access, scald-proof faucets, articulated shower heads, and hardware for arthritic fingers. With all of these options available, each facility area should be reviewed to ensure accommodations have been made for mobility- and dexterity-impaired individuals.

MECHANICAL EQUIPMENT CONSIDERATIONS

As the ability to move quickly decreases with age, elevator doors and other automatic equipment must be adjusted to accommodate slower response times. Emergency equipment, especially exits, must facilitate easy use.

The new frontier in our world of daily life is inner space. Much can be done in the creation of small spaces to give a feeling of comfort, interest, and value. Sitting areas in corridors or adjacent to activity spaces, as well as card rooms, libraries, and craft space, are good examples of small, comfortable, interesting spaces. This is a useful marketing tool for owners and developers.

REFERENCES

Brown, N. 1989. A Sense of Space. *Designer's West*. October: 106.
Spence, A. 1988. *Biology of Human Aging*. Englewood Cliffs, N.J.: Prentice-Hall.

SUGGESTED READINGS

Abramovice, B. 1988. *Long-Term Care Administration*. New York: The Haworth Press.
Brukoff, B. 1989. Manifesto: Against Cerebral Design. *Designer's West*. August: 166.
Design for Aging: An Architect's Guide. 1985. Washington, D.C.: AIA Press.
Dychtwald, K., and Flower, J. 1989. *Age Wave*. Los Angeles: Jeremy P. Tarcher, Inc.
Erickson, J. 1988. *Wisdom and the Senses*. New York: W. W. Norton.
Gordon, P. 1988. *Developing Retirement Facilities*. New York: John Wiley & Sons.
Olgay, N. 1989. Wayfinding—Creating Accessible Environments. *Designer's West*. July: 122–26.
Ward, A. 1984. *The Aging Experience*. New York: Harper and Row.
Wolfe, D. 1990. *Serving the Ageless Market*. New York: McGraw Hill.

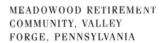

MEADOWOOD RETIREMENT COMMUNITY, VALLEY FORGE, PENNSYLVANIA

The main lobby corridor functions as the circulation axis of the facility, which is a thoroughfare of pedestrian circulation linking the assisted living center, skilled nursing facility, congregate living units, and community center. The traditional detailing with columns and keystone arches reflects the design essence of the project. (Architecture: CS&D Architects; interiors: Life Designs; photo: Michael Schoenfeld.)

CHAPTER TWO

TYPES OF RETIREMENT FACILITIES

THE ROSSMOOR REGENCY,
LAGUNA BEACH,
CALIFORNIA

A hexagonal pavilion in the middle of the Regency's Tropical Courtyard serves as the entertainment center. Commons spaces—the dining room, lobby, and lobby lounge—are oriented toward courtyard views. Lush tropical landscaping over much of the site features ferns, palms, and evergreens. (Architecture: Terry Architects; landscape architecture: Forsum/Summers & Partners, Inc.; photo: Milroy/McAleer.)

The different types of environments used to describe retirement housing seem infinite in number, and they often overlap so closely that characterizing them distinctly can be next to impossible. There are many differences of opinion regarding the names of senior facilities, with *retirement village* and *nursing home* spanning the spectrum of positive-associated to negative-associated terms. Until recently, the five facility types considered for seniors housing, in ascending order of breadth of services provided, were:

- Elderly housing
- Senior/community centers
- Residential care facilities
- Nursing homes
- Continuing care retirement communities

Housing for the elderly began in 939 A.D. in the English almshouses, which were provided by the church and clustered around the church and its attendant buildings. While this early example shows housing for the elderly beginning with financial support from a source other than the residents of the housing, the advent of *private* funding for housing, or housing being paid for by the residents, is a relatively new phenomenon. This shift to the private sector will continue to change the type of housing that will be demanded by the seniors market.

Paul Gordon, of the law firm of Hanson, Bridgett, Marcus, Vlahos, and Rudy in San Francisco, illustrates the hybrid nature of the contemporary retirement center. Indeed, as he details, it combines various facets of a skilled nursing facility, a pure housing subdivision, an apartment, a high-rise residential building, and a condominium (Gordon 1988, 26–27):

Centers for the elderly have evolved along two separate paths, with housing as the genesis of one, and health and custodial care at the source of the other. With time, these two branches have intertwined so much that retirement centers currently are thought of as places that are neither pure housing nor pure care, but a little of each, and a lot of added service and amenities that form the middle ground. . . .

Over the years, many different models of retirement facilities have developed that incorporate some mixture of housing, convenience services, care, or insurance. Principally, these fall into three basic patterns: congregate housing, board and care, and continuing care or life care. . . . These traditional points of departure are becoming arbitrary stereotypes that do not fit the marketplace.

ST. CATHERINE'S VILLAGE, MADISON, MISSISSIPPI

TOP LEFT: The roofline is distinguished by its 95-foot-high (29-meter-high) steeple. (Architecture and interiors: Cooke Douglass Farr, Ltd.; photo: John O'Hagan.)

TOP RIGHT: Residents can sit in the inner portion of the porte-cochere, which leads directly to the lobby. (Architecture and interiors: Cooke Douglass Farr, Ltd.; photo: John O'Hagan.)

RIGHT: The airy chapel is grounded by forest-green carpeting. A small space sectioned off by columns on the right provides privacy for intimate gatherings. (Architecture and interiors: Cooke Douglass Farr, Ltd.; custom altar furniture: Fletcher Cox; carpet: Shaw Industries; paint: Benjamin Moore; wallcovering: Maharam; seating: David Edward with Unika Vaev fabric; photo: John O'Hagan.)

While health and security are important considerations, it is likely that the facilities that previously focused on care-giving and lower-level needs will be replaced in the near future by facilities designed to satisfy the higher-level needs of self-actualization, wisdom, and experience. Indeed, the seniors occupying these upscale facilities will expect a more sophisticated physical design package, a more broad-ranging services package, and personnel who will satisfy their need for self-esteem.

The types of services packages provided in retirement facilities stem from the wide variety of different services needed for older adults, ranging from simple information and referral services to complex health-care services. To describe every combination of service options within this range would be virtually impossible. As we isolate primary points along the retirement facility spectrum, we can isolate the most common facility types being developed today. Of course, this spectrum of facilities designed for older adults is dynamic and will continue to change as the market redefines its needs.

INDEPENDENT HOUSING

Independent living can range from an entire "new town," a village or a small subdivision with freestanding home sites or condominiums with little or no services, to a congregate setting with a full range of services.

DETACHED DWELLING. Popular among many primary retirees is the concept of *detached dwelling units*. These units may be situated adjacent to congregate housing units on a campus, or clustered in neighborhoods throughout a campus (congregate communities are larger facilities that include a mix of housing types, including attached houses, congregate houses, and a congregate apartment hotel). They may consist of duplex or fourplex dwellings, individual cottages, or garden homes. The advantages of living in a detached dwelling unit are similar to those of condominium living: The resident enjoys complete independent living, yet also has the benefits of a menu of services available on an as-needed basis, including dining services, social and recreational services,

WHITE HORSE VILLAGE,
EDGEMONT TOWNSHIP,
PENNSYLVANIA

Carpeting in the lobby keys the color scheme of the Village's commons spaces. (Architecture: Bower Lewis Thrower/Architects; interiors: Merlino Interior Design; carpet: U.S. Axminster; furniture: Weiman Co., D. Becker & Sons; fabric: Kravet Fabrics; drapery fabric: Dazian's Inc.; drapery workroom: Drapery Etc.; artwork: Galman, Lepow Associates; silk trees, plants: Foliage Design; painting: S. W. Kooperman; accessories: Landsman Gallery; photo: Richard Quindry.)

educational programs, and so on. Other significant advantages are the upkeep of common landscaping and the availability of commons facilities for resident use. Many facilities also feature on-campus health services in a step-down care setting. This combines the freedom to lock the door and leave for work or pleasure with a tremendous resource of convenience, services, and amenities. Depending on the target market, the size and quality of detached living units will vary. Generally, they are single-level and smaller than the homes from which their residents have come.

Many of the larger communities provide a full range of opportunities for recreation and sports centered around an activities center. When there are different levels of care within a retirement community, activity centers should be separated by resident type—independent-living, assisted-living, or skilled-care. However, research suggests that such advanced physical provisions as swimming pools and fitness and exercise facilities are not important variables for seniors making relocation decisions.

Each independent living unit in a congregate setting has its own living space with a kitchen or kitchenette and a complete bathroom. Individual washers and dryers, while helpful, do not seem to be important in the design of senior housing—except for a resident's need to project independence. Many independent living units provide personal emergency response systems integrated into the facility's security scheme, an important determinant for seniors. Services offered by a majority of retirement centers that are considered top choices are food and beverage service (which may include up to three meals per day); social programs, recreation services, and activities, including group or individual travel planning, exercise clubs, craft clubs, and card clubs; transportation; and community outreach organizations, such as Gray Ladies, or the Service Core of Retired Executives. Additional amenities that also rate as essential include meeting rooms and libraries, convenience stores, a chapel, and beauty and barber salons. Less essential amenities might include pharmacies, flower and plant shops, gift and antique shops, financial institutions, and other retail stores.

Medical services may be provided as well. Physicians, dentists, and other medical providers typically use space provided by the facility to see patients. These medical providers may or may not be on staff at the facility itself.

CONGREGATE LIVING. The program and services packages for congregate living imposes few limitations to residents' freedom, with the residents' independence of paramount concern. In fact, regular dining service and transportation may be the only services that a congregate living facility resident may share with other residents. Many tenants within congregate living units provide for themselves fully in a setting that is much like normal apartment or condominium living. Most residents of congregate living units maintain very active life-styles and outside interests. Many move into a congregate living facility for security and convenience reasons.

These units vary in size from 650 to 2,500 square feet (60 to 232 square meters). They may comprise single, double, or triple bedroom units. All have at least one bathroom, a kitchen, a dining/living area, and sometimes a den or laundry area. Some residents use a spare bedroom as a den or craft room that may also double as a guest room. Most congregate living units are unfurnished, which allows residents the opportunity to completely personalize their own space. Parking space is usually provided for residents' cars, since most still own and use their own automobiles.

Most residents of congregate living units engage in social, recreational, and educational programs offered on a facility's campus. Many are active in leadership, and organize programmed activities for their peers, including volunteerism in retail store management, library sciences, gardening, grounds conservation, arts and crafts, music, exercise and dance instruction, university extension classes, and outside community services.

INDEPENDENT LIVING. This type of living arrangement allows individuals the option of independently managing their own small but private living unit. Area per unit may vary, but an average independent living unit is usually between 1,000 and 2,000 square feet (93 and 186 square meters). This type of unit always includes a bedroom, bathroom, and living room area; most also include a kitchenette/dining area.

THE FORUM AT DEER CREEK, DEERFIELD BEACH, FLORIDA

The formal parlor flows into the more casual women's card room. (Architecture: Helman Hurley, Charvat Peacock. interiors: ABV & Associates, Inc.; carved armchairs: Kreiss with Robert Allen fabric; lamp tables: Cal Mode; sofa: Wesley Hall with Stroheim & Romann fabric; cocktail table: Baker Knapp & Tubbs; lounge chairs: Wesley Hall with Coraggio fabric; armoire: Hekman; chandelier: Tom Thumb Lighting; lamps: Remington, Markel; plants: Plant Worksl carpet: Shaw Industries; artwork: Art Dallas; photo: Peter Paige.)

THE SEASONS KENWOOD, CINCINNATI, OHIO

TOP: Clad in rosy brick, The Seasons is laid out on a cruciform plan, with residential wings radiating from the atrium lobby. (Architecture: PDT + Co.; interiors: Lynn Wilson Associates, Inc.; photo: Eric Hecktor.)

CENTER, BOTTOM: Residents at The Seasons have a choice of three different one- and two-bedroom apartment plans, each with carpeting, a fully equipped kitchen, and individual outdoor terraces. Lynn Wilson designed the model bedroom and the sitting room in cheerful pastels. (Architecture: PDT + Co.; interiors: Lynn Wilson Associates, Inc.; bedroom model unit—headboard, nightstand, dresser, wall mirror: American of Martinsville; lounge chair: Drexel Heritage with fabric by Stroheim & Romann; fabric for coverlet, dust ruffle, and draperies: Kravel, lamps: Remington Lamp; wallcovering: Kinney Contract Wallcovering; carpet: Durkan Patterned Carpet; sitting room model unit—carpet: Durkan Patterned Carpet; wallcovering: Kinney Contract Wallcovering; sofa, desk, desk chair, occasional table: Drexel; sofa fabric: Stroheim & Romann; desk chair fabric: F. Schumacher; desk and floor lamps: Paul Hanson; shutters: Barry Farmer; photo: Eric Hecktor.)

The purpose of an independent living unit is to promote independence and individuality among residents. In facilities where meals are provided in a common dining area, residents may be encouraged to prepare their own meals. Where units with kitchenettes are offered, it is sometimes preferable or advisable for residents to do some of their own meal preparation, to foster independence. Standardized architectural finishes are often offered, but units are otherwise unfurnished, and residents are encouraged to bring their own furnishings to personalize their spaces (although some facilities provide furniture, both to service the residents and to generate additional revenue for the facility via rental fees). Many facilities also offer weekly laundry service for bed linen, but residents are encouraged to do their own personal laundry in available centralized facilities on the premises. Each campus may also offer a variety of other amenities, including transportation, social activities, recreational activities, paid utilities (except telephone), and so forth.

CONTINUING CARE RETIREMENT COMMUNITIES (CCRCs)

Full-service CCRCs (also frequently referred to as *lifecare communities*) provide an entire range of services, including independent living, assisted living, skilled nursing (sometimes contracted to a skilled nursing home operator), and, in some situations, hospice (a special residential facility for the terminally ill, providing for individual physical and emotional needs as well as for family emotional concerns). Many support services, such as activities, a fitness/health club, and so forth, and a full range of medical services are provided.

CCRCs can range from communities of detached housing to apartments in an urban high-rise or other single building to clustered buildings in a campuslike setting. In full-service CCRCs, "the contract provides for full or lifetime health care as needed at no substantial increase above the monthly payments made in the independent living unit."

THE SEASONS KENWOOD, CINCINNATI, OHIO

The furniture and the strong but soothing pattern of the carpet provides good visual contrast. (Architecture: PDT + Co.; interiors: Lynn Wilson Associates, Inc.; carpet: Durkan Patterned Carpet; armchair: Bernhardt Industries with Stroheim & Romann fabric; side chair: Bernhardt Industries with Kravet fabric; lounge chair: Drexel Heritage with P/Kaufmann fabric; oval coffee table: Casa Stradivari; other tables, credenza, and benches: Drexel Heritage; mirrors: Bartet Imports; sconces: Champion Lighting; table lamps: Frederick Cooper Lamps; photo: Eric Hecktor.)

CARLETON-WILLARD
VILLAGE, BEDFORD,
MASSACHUSETTS

TOP: Bright yellow paint is used in the atrium to heighten the excitement of the space. Accenting the walls of Main Street and the atrium are reproductions of antique French lamps. (Architecture: TRO/The Ritchie Organization; interiors: Adner/Woodman Design; photo: Robert Mikrut.)

BOTTOM: Floor plan. Legend: 1. Auditorium. 2. Atrium. 3. Arts and crafts room. 4. Billiard room. 5. Offices. 6. Snack bar. 7. Café seating. 8. Corridor to dining room. 9. Main Street. 10. Lounge seating. 11. General store. (Architecture: TRO/The Ritchie Organization.)

If the resident depletes his or her financial resources, the CCRC assumes the burden of payment" (Zeisel and Burkart 1989). *Modified-service CCRCs* provide for a guaranteed limited number of paid days in a nursing home bed, and *fee-for-service CCRCs*, while guaranteeing a nursing home bed, require that residents pay full per-diem rates.

RESIDENTIAL CARE OR ASSISTED LIVING FACILITIES (ALFs)

Residential care facilities are primarily regulated institutions. While not every state is regulated, each state has its own designation for licensed residential care facilities, and the names used to describe such homes include domiciliary, foster, group, institution, personal, community, minimum, adult, supervisory, alternative, rest, congregate, shelter, intermediate, adult congregate, and so forth. These types of facilities can range from formal organizations to smaller, informal organizations of individuals who come together for housing, foodservice, and a low level of care and activities of daily living (ADL). Depending on the type of facility and the state in which it is located, it may have to be licensed.

Residents have their own private apartments in the assisted living model, and may share living space in the other residential care models. These facilities do not ordinarily provide for nursing services, but do include activities of daily living—transportation services, walking, climbing or descending stairs, eating, dressing, bathing, toileting, and other personal hygiene and grooming needs, reminders to take (but not administering of) medication, transferring in and out of beds and chairs, general correspondence, financial management, and other personal needs.

An assisted living facility may be freestanding or be an element of a CCRC, a lifecare community, or an adult retirement community. Assisted living facilities (ALFs) within larger adult retirement communities are becoming necessary, as managers have realized that

THE FORUM AT OVERLAND PARK, KANSAS

ABOVE: French-influenced details and a rich color scheme create a dramatic first impression in the lobby. (Architecture: National Architectural Services; interiors: I.D.A.; sofa, wing chairs: Henredon with Brunschwig & Fils fabric; side chairs: Lambert, Henredon with Robert Allen, Duralee fabrics; bookcase: Henredon; brass chest: Sarreid; floor lamps: Paul Hanson; nesting tables: Sherrill; lamp: Remington; sofa table/desk: Pflasters/Zimports; loveseats: Beverly with Brunschwig & Fils fabric; cocktail table: Beverly; Carpet: Shaw Industries, Patcraft; floors: Permagrain; wallcovering: Kinney Contract; end table: Wellington Hall; photo: Tom Sanders/Architectural Fotographics.)

RIGHT: Thanks to the L shape of the skilled-care living room, television watchers don't disturb residents gathered for conversation.

(Architecture: National Architectural Services; interiors: I.D.A.; side chairs: Henredon Furniture with P/Kaufmann fabric; sofa: St. Timothy with Gilford, Kravet fabric; end table: Henredon Furniture; lamps: David Thomas, Kaiser Kuhn; drapery: P/Kaufmann, fabricated by Sherrill Draperies; carpet: Mannington Carpets-Wellco; wallcovering: Sunwall; photo: Tom Sanders/Architectural Fotographics.)

alternatives to a skilled nursing facility had to be offered. ALFs provide step-down care instead of the high level of care that must be offered in a skilled nursing facility. ALFs tend to be smaller than independent living units, and many communities have converted their efficiency units to ALFs when design and layout offer the option. In other communities, ALFs have been redesigned as residents have *aged in place* (an industry term for the aging process and the design and/or management efforts to accommodate it). With the addition of home health care, ALFs are beginning to compete with nursing homes, skilled nursing facilities, and other long-term care facilities. In these situations, the license is held by the agency delivering medical services, while the facility itself provides only housing and foodservice.

The purpose of an ALF living arrangement is to aid an individual in maintaining as much independence and freedom as possible, except for periodic assistance with such specific tasks as bathing, dressing, medication dosage, transportation and similar needs. The advantage of assisted living is that

multiple residents can share common services, and the costs thereof, to meet common needs. These services may include meals, transportation, periodic nursing, security, housekeeping, and so on. Many ALF residents may still be fully capable of cooking (although this is usually not allowed in most ALF environments), housekeeping, and self-transportation, and may choose to continue providing these services for themselves as long as possible.

Within the structure of the assisted living program, a certified nursing assistant or licensed professional nurse (LPN) is required to make three daily rounds of the residents' units to make a security check as well as to offer assistance with areas of task specific need.

In some ALF housing developments, resident units are identical to independent living units; in others, unit size is made smaller by the deletion of the kitchen/dining areas, which may decrease unit size by as much as 150 to 200 square feet (14 to 19 square meters). Most residences are one-bedroom units with a living room and bathroom. Many are fully or partially furnished.

NURSING HOMES AND SKILLED NURSING FACILITIES (SNFs)

An SNF is a facility dedicated to the maintenance of the life-style quality and health care needs of multiple individuals within a setting of commonly shared services, such as bathing, dressing, meal service, social, recreational, and educational programs, medication, and so forth. Skilled nursing units may be part of a larger campus of a congregate living setting, offering the availability of step-down care for temporary convalescing to campus residents. For this reason, the much more appropriate and positive title of *health center* or *nursing center* has been given to many of these types of facilities. These are offered as a convenience and security feature in the total package of campus amenities.

Nursing homes are highly regulated, and the SNF model is relatively standard across the United States. SNFs are licensed facilities staffed with licensed administrators, and offer a full range of long-term-care medical services. Regulations require that a certain number of

MEADOWOOD RETIREMENT
COMMUNITY, VALLEY
FORGE, PENNSYLVANIA

LEFT: The main dining room seats 250 and serves two meals a day. Its English Country theme works well against a backdrop of green Pennsylvania hills, seen through the generous windows. (Architecture: CS&D Architects; interiors: Life Designs; carpet: Burtco; chairs: Stanley; tables, planters: Granite Mill; fabrics: Grayson; drapery: La Bai; lighting fixtures: Chapman, CSL; photo: Michael Schoenfeld.)

THE FORUM AT
OVERLAND PARK, KANSAS

BELOW: Upscale decorative touches, such as the Welsh dresser and copper pots, carry a residential ambience into the skilled care dining room. (Architecture: National Architectural Services; interiors: I.D.A.; chairs: Shelby Williams with fabric by Duralee, Naugahyde; wallcovering: Sellers & Josephson; photo: Tom Sanders/Architectural Fotographics.)

registered nurses (RNs), licensed practical nurses (LPNs), licensed vocational nurses (LVNs), and nursing assistants or aides be on staff. The required size of the staff depends on the degree of care required by the residents. Sometimes floors or wings of the facility are designated for specified levels of care.

SNFs are designed to provide round-the-clock care to meet all health-related, psychological, and other personal and medical needs of residents requiring constant care. The services of an RN are available seven days per week and 24 hours per day. The types of individuals who become residents of SNFs do not require the acute level of care delivered by hospitals, and SNFs do service rehabilitative, substance abuse, and psychologically dependent patients requiring long-term maintenance or shorter-term rehabilitative medical care.

For most senior residents, the move to a skilled nursing unit signals a more permanently dependent and final stage of life. The very term *skilled nursing* conjures images of dread and apprehension. Historically, the image of the convalescent home has had connotations of

dreary, unkempt, and malodorous surroundings. In attempting to counteract this stereotype, many skilled nursing units today share the common goal of offering residents dignity and purpose in living in spite of their residence in an institutional setting. Skilled nursing residents are usually housed in private (single-occupancy) or semiprivate (double-occupancy) rooms. Although SNF residence tends to be long-term, it is not acute or even subacute in nature.

The average amount of space allotted for a resident's personal area in an SNF is approximately 150 square feet (14 square meters) for each patient in a semiprivate room, and 280 square feet (26 square meters) in a private room. These areas will vary in requirement from state to state, and local codes that may allow as little as 80 square feet (7.4 square meters) per patient in a semiprivate room and 150 square feet (14 square meters) in a private unit. Generally, these rooms are furnished with furniture by the facility. Residents are sometimes encouraged to bring their own favorite chair, dresser, cabinet, or artwork. Each unit consists of a bedroom with an attached toilet room,

BROOKHAVEN AT
LEXINGTON, LEXINGTON,
MASSACHUSETTS

Soft-hued walls, carpeting, and
chair upholstery provide a serene
background for the floral fabric of
the draperies, bedspreads, and
upholstered headboards in the
bedroom. Privacy curtains hang
unobtrusively when retracted.
(Architecture: Russell Gibson von
Dohlen; interiors: Arthur Shuster,
Inc.; draperies, bedspreads: Saul
Siegal Fabric; cubicle curtain:
DesignTex; casegoods: American
of Martinsville; custom
headboard: Randy's Interiors with
Saul Siegal Fabric; lounge chair:
Southland Furniture Co. with
Genon fabric; lamps: Remington
Lamps; carpet: Atlas Carpets;
photo: A. F. Payne Photographic.)

MEADOWOOD RETIREMENT
COMMUNITY, VALLEY
FORGE, PENNSYLVANIA

LEFT: Resident beds are offset
in a toe to toe position in this
semiprivate room, which features
a nontraditional approach to
room layout. All casework was
custom-designed to work with the
room scale. Finishes were kept
light-valued to increase perceived
spaciousness. (Architect: CS&D
Architects; interiors: Life Designs;
photo: Michael Schoenfeld.)

which will often contain a shower for
bathing, depending on the abilities
of each resident. A common bathing
room is also available to help those who
have difficulty bathing themselves.
A staff member assists these individuals in bathing, as they cannot
be left unattended.

All SNF meals are served in a common dining room, which can accommodate normal and handicapped dining.
New OBRA laws require that choice for
dining location be given to residents. Although meals are served at bedside to
those who are not ambulatory, most residents are encouraged to leave their
rooms for dining and other functions,
such as social and recreational activities,
thus promoting independence.

Residents usually enter a skilled
nursing facility when the regular need
for medical attention becomes burdensome to maintain under normal living
conditions. The daily availability and attention of a nursing staff and, when required, physician's services, lessen this
medical burden for the individuals and
their families. SNFs normally range in
size from 40 to 250 beds. Residential
wings are usually attached to a common
core of services, such as dining, social,

and recreational services, physical therapy, common bathing, and so on. Many
facilities also offer transportation, allowing their residents to participate in occasional outside community activities.
Some facilities also arrange for outside
community social and educational organizations to offer extension programs,
which are brought in for residents.

ALZHEIMER'S AND SPECIALTY UNITS

In terms of basic services offered, these
units are similar to skilled nursing units.
Their individual designs, however, are
specialized according to the specific conditions or infirmities of the patient population they will be serving.

When discussing Alzheimer's units, it
is worth noting that the term *Alzheimer's
Disease* has been given to a range of maladies that actually encompasses about 20
different conditions of dementia, each
with its own specific traits and symptoms. Two general conditions of this
range are periods of complete disorientation to physical surroundings and
periodic fits of restlessness, rage, or
reclusion.

LA POSADA AT PARK CENTRE, GREEN VALLEY, ARIZONA

Administrators of skilled nursing facilities like dining rooms that can practically be hosed down, but easy-to-clean, hard surfaces also bounce sound around too much. To compensate for this, the dining room employs banners to soften the noise level and provide color. (Architecture: Englebrecht and Griffin; interiors: Life Designs; wall murals: Winfield; stacking dining chairs: Thonet with canvaslike vinyl by AAT; table: Amisco legs support a CHF top; flooring: Armstrong; photo: Ed Rosenberger.)

FAIRWAYS AT BROOKLINE VILLAGE, STATE COLLEGE, PENNSYLVANIA

TOP LEFT: The light-filled solariums, like this one with its pale wood furnishings, plants, and flower-dotted wallcovering, are cheerful surroundings in which to visit. (Architecture: Robert L. Beers, AIA, Architects; interiors: Merlino Interior Design Associates; carpet: Bigelow; wallcovering: Sanitas Wallcovering; fabrics: Coral of Chicago; furniture: Thonet; photo Richard Quindry.)

BOTTOM LEFT: In the nursing care units, soft colors, flowered wallpaper, and turned head- and footboards help to diminish the "nursing home" atmosphere. (Architecture: Robert L. Beers, AIA, Architects; interiors: Merlino Interior Design Associates; carpet: Lees Carpet; fabrics: DesignTex; wallcovering: Sanitas Wallcovering; furniture: Joerns, Thonet, Amedco; artwork: Franklin Picture Co.; photo: Richard Quindry.)

Senile dementia, or simply dementia, is one of the two major types of chronic brain syndrome affecting older people (the other is depression). Fifty to 75 percent of dementia cases are due to Alzheimer's Disease. In clinical terms, dementia is characterized by the progressive deterioration of cognitive functions, usually accompanied by changes in emotions and personality. Moreover, Alzheimer's patients may have periodic fits of violence and extreme fluctuations of emotional behavior. It is not uncommon for them to be unable to recognize their family or friends. Many such patients wander aimlessly and are often unable to attend to simple daily tasks of personal care and hygiene. The causes of dementia, unfortunately, are varied and ill-defined.

The extent of severe dementia among elderly people is estimated to range from 1 to 6 percent of the elderly population. The prevalence of dementia increases markedly with age, so that by the age of 80, one-fifth of the population is stricken with dementia, and 17 percent have Alzheimer's Disease. The Alzheimer's figure increases to 30 percent among those 85 and older.

Because many dementia patients are confused and may misinterpret some visual cues, it is important that the design of the unit be simple, to allow patients freedom of mobility and a minimum of anxiety. An uncomplicated physical layout is essential. Because confusion among Alzheimer's patients can trigger episodes of anger when a door, window, or corridor is not where it "should" be, it is important to create a design where patients cannot harm themselves. Experienced planners should consult with medical personnel who specialize in this area before finalizing solutions in the design plan for Alzheimer's units.

The general layout of an Alzheimer's unit will often be shaped in a square or as a straight, long plan; it may also include a commons quadrant. Each plan offers residents a simple, direct, unconfusing pathway to walk without getting lost. As is sometimes required by law, it is very worthwhile to provide a fenced outdoor activity space for the Alzheimer's residents.

Depending on the specialty of a unit, certain additional criteria must be considered in design solutions. For instance, the considerations for dementia might include:

1. Simplicity in verbiage and symbols on site signage

2. A lack of potentially dangerous objects, such as tripping and tangling hazards with floor surfaces, drapery cords, electrical appliances and outlets that present a risk of electrocution, and so on
3. Simplicity and ease in location and use of light switches, grab bars and handrails, appliances, faucets, showers, and toilets
4. Use of furnishings that are impervious to abuse and incontinence, such as tight seat bottoms and back rests, cleanable surfaces wherever possible, smooth edges, and counterweighted case goods and tables
5. An adequate line of sight and surveillance points for staff and patients, to provide a constant means of orientation of place

FEE STRUCTURES

Fee structures for residence in a retirement facility can range from a large entrance fee or endowment with a small monthly maintenance fee to no entrance fee or endowment and a traditional lease or straight monthly rental—no different than one would pay to rent an apartment. Another alternative would include

THE RENAISSANCE, AUSTIN, TEXAS

Residents walking by the card room can see what's going on inside, thanks to a series of arched openings along perimeter walls, which also provide plenty of light. (Architecture: Good Fulton & Farrell; interiors: ABV & Associates; carpet: Porter Carpet Mill; window treatments: Sherrill Draperies; fabrics: Robert Allen, John Edward Hughes; card chairs: Custom ABV Design/Stylerite Furniture; card tables: Hekman; photo: Peter Paige.)

a form of real estate ownership, which could include a condominium, cooperative, or outright ownership arrangement, and each of these ownership options could include a monthly services fee.

RENTAL. In the 1960s and 1970s the trend in retirement facilities was toward the *life-care model*. Under this form of housing, an individual assigned his or her assets from a currently owned home to a facility or organization, which in turn agreed to house the individual and provide medical and nutritional maintenance requirements for the remainder of the individual's life. This arrangement, while good in concept, allowed no latitude for a later reversal of the individual's decision. Moreover, many organizations found that a resident's assets rarely covered overhead in the long run.

The *rental model*, which began to come into greater use in the 1980s, affords all parties the opportunity for economic freedom in a changing market and provides a flexible setting for changing life-style conditions during step-down care. Under the many rental scenarios of various facilities, the individual may be required to post a large deposit—usually from around $40,000 to $60,000—upon entry, although this condition significantly reduces a retirement facility's market competitiveness. In some facilities, this sum is deposited in an interest-bearing account, with a portion of the interest usually kept by the facility and sometimes given to the individual. This deposit provides an assurance that services can continue for a significant period of time, even if the individual's income is seriously impaired. This also gives the individual time to make other housing arrangements without it becoming an immediate emergency. The interest from deposit, coupled with monthly rental fees of the house, apartment unit, or room, usually offsets the cost of providing services and physical amenities. At the end of a resident's stay, the original deposit is usually refunded to the resident or his or her surviving family.

THE RENAISSANCE,
SHERMAN, TEXAS

Rich, dark woods stand out against pale wall tones in the billiard room, a favorite place to socialize. (Architecture: Archon; interiors: ABV & Associates; billiard table: Fort Worth Billiards; poker table, card table: Romweber; poker and card chair: Charlotte Chair with Charlotte Chair vinyl; carpet: Contract Carpets, Mohawk; chandelier: Hart; wallcovering: Genon with Sterling Prints border; photo: Peter Paige.)

CLASSIC RESIDENCE
BY HYATT,
TEANECK, NEW JERSEY

Residents gather in the cozy restaurant lounge before meals. (Architecture: Fusco, Shaffer & Pappas, Inc.; interiors: Culpepper, McAuliffe and Meaders, Inc.; carpet: Trafford Park Carpets; seating: Custom Craft, Hospitality Furniture Company, Shelby Williams; fabric: Donghia, Payne Fabrics; tables: Murray's Iron Works, Houseparts; lamps: Kostka; chandelier: Alger Lighting; drapery: Unlimited Design Resource; photo: Gabriel Benzur.)

THE RENAISSANCE,
AUSTIN, TEXAS

The main parlor is a relaxing place to watch television and socialize. (Architecture: Good Fulton & Farrell; interioren: ABV & Associates; carpet: Porter Carpet Mill; sofas: Custom ABV Design/Jesus Marroquin Workroom; armchairs: JAG International; cocktail and sofa tables: Bausman; Accessories: Crandale Galleries; photo: Peter Paige.)

Most rental situations include daily meals, flat laundry service, daily transportation, full use of social, recreational, and educational facilities and programs, and a certain number of sick days (usually 30) per year covered under a campus health services plan. These are generally offered as a menu of services in the upper-middle and upper-income markets.

OWNERSHIPS. As an outgrowth of the health-care field, retirement housing has traditionally been structured on a rental-based system. Heavy emphasis on provided services (especially health care) has, until recently, demanded that the developer/owner/manager rent rather than sell space for resident occupancy. But with the passing of the Tax Reform Act of 1986, the purchase option has also become more popular. The following example illustrates this point:

- Current typical market value of a home: $300,000

- Original purchase price: $25,000
- Improvements: $25,000
- One-time senior exemption: $125,000
- Capital gain tax liability: $125,000

By selling a home and reinvesting the capital gain in another real estate purchase as a primary residence, an individual saves paying taxes on $125,000 even with the one-time exemption allowed for seniors by the tax law.

One potential difficulty here is that the facility owner may not be able to maintain sufficient control over the development once it comes under the control of a home-owners association. Owners and developers have negotiated with such associations for exclusive management contract rights to provide services to the residents, but the law now prohibits this. A developer wishing to maintain control of the operation is not on sound footing to do so, given the unpredictable whims of these associations.

If the developer also wishes to be the operator, the alternative is to retain a certain percentage of the space in the development under the developer's control. The choices might allow for a split rental/ownership option for residents, with the developer owning (and renting or leasing) a sufficient number of units to maintain control of sufficient home-owners-association votes to award the management contract to the operator (that is, to him- or herself). Another option is for the developer to retain ownership of the public space, the retail space, the dining areas, and so forth, with the voting rights allocated according to area instead of on a per-unit basis. Yet another method is to create a club that the residents join as part of their living in the community, with the owner/developer retaining ownership of the *public* space, which the residents are then allowed to use in exchange for a monthly "club membership" fee.

Perhaps the thorniest issue under the ownership model involves the removal of a resident for violation of the resident agreement (such as for having a child of

THE RENAISSANCE,
SHERMAN, TEXAS

LEFT: A graceful colonnade lends presence to the main lobby. (Architecture: Archon; interiors: ABV & Associates; wall sconces: Stonetech; chandelier: Hart; tile floor: Fiandre; carpet: Contract Carpet, Carrera Custom Graphic; lounge Chairs, armchairs: Massoud Custom Furniture with fabric by Bassett McNab; sofas: Massoud Custom Furniture with fabric by Maharam; table: Michael Hamilton; photo: Peter Paige.)

RIGHT: Just off the lobby, a cozy living room invites relaxation. (Architecture: Archon; interiors: ABV & Associates; desk: Cal-Mode; lounge chair: Massoud Custom furniture with Counterpoint Mardi Gras fabric; sofa: Massoud Custom furniture with Robert Allen fabric; cocktail table: Cal-Mode; arm chair: Shelby Williams with Pindler & Pindler fabric; photo: Peter Paige.)

the resident move in) or because the resident is no longer capable of living independently. After a probationary period, how easily can management evict a resident when the resident owns the accommodations?

Generally an entrance fee or endowment is required as a means of reducing the monthly maintenance fee associated with ownership. Endowments may be either refundable (in full or in part) or nonrefundable. Using 1 percent per month as a rule of thumb for the amount of money an investment (or endowment, in this case) can spin off, an initial endowment of $200,000 would spin off $2,000 per month. If the management company determined that the selling price of a particular apartment, including the services package, could be marketed (or would cost the management company/owner/developer) at $3,500 per month, then the resident would only be required to pay a $1,500 monthly maintenance fee (that is $3,500 less $2,000 from the entrance fee or endowment).

A distinction needs to be made between the entrance fee or endowment and the monthly rental structure with regard to the benefits for the owner/developer. The owner/developer incurs substantial debt in developing a retirement center. In addition to the traditional expenses involved in developing a $100 million project, the developer of a retirement center must endure an unusually lengthy period of time in securing appropriate zoning approvals (and certificates of need, if required by law). The average time from inception to 95% stabilized occupancy for the average retirement center is nine years. This long time period is due to several factors: the fact that

prime locations are in residential rather than commercial zones (with abutters who tend to be particularly sensitive to multiunit housing in their neighborhoods); the hybrid nature of a retirement center—neither purely residential nor purely commercial; the relative infancy of the retirement industry; and the perceived novelty of retirement centers by the general public.

Given these factors, the investor group supporting the developer may be encouraged to sell residential units rather than rent them, thereby recovering the investment more rapidly than by amortizing the debt over a longer period, and using the rental income to retire the debt.

Another key issue is the security of the entrance fee or endowment. Owners and developers have developed methods to overcome these concerns by offering full or partial refunds of the investments. This technique can be particularly beneficial for successful retirement developments—a retirement center with a long resident waiting list can easily promise refunds and then provide references in the form of former residents (or the executors of former residents' estates who have had their endowments or entrance fees reimbursed).

The issue of *imputed interest* will have an impact on the marketability of refundable endowment or entrance fees. With the large number of for-profit developers and owners entering the retirement housing industry and coupling housing with service packages, the exemption for qualified continuing care retirement facilities is becoming blurred. The Internal Revenue Service considers a *refundable* entrance fee or endowment

(or the refundable portion of the entrance fee or endowment) either as a loan from the resident to the owner/developer or as prepaid rent. In the case of a loan, the resident must treat at least some of the interest on the refundable portion, even though not received, as income, and is liable for taxes thereon. The amount of this taxable interest, termed "imputed interest," is determined by the Secretary of the Treasury. Under current tax laws, the first $90,000 of such imputed interest is tax-exempt, so long as the facility meets certain criteria.

If the entrance or endowment fee is considered as prepaid rent, the owner/developer is required to pay taxes on the amount, since it would be considered taxable rent income. Indeed, the *non*refundable portion is considered as income to the developer and as a corresponding expense to the resident.

REFERENCES

Design for Aging: An Architect's Guide. 1985. Washington, D.C.: AIA Press.

Goldman. J. n.d. *Dictionary of Terms for Senior Citizens and the Industries That Serve Them.* Annapolis: The National Association for Senior Living Industries.

Gordon, P. 1988. *Developing Retirement Facilities.* New York: John Wiley & Sons.

Zeisel, J., and Burkart, D. n.d. *Dictionary of Terms for Senior Citizens and the Industries That Serve Them.* Annapolis: The National Association for Senior Living Industries.

SUGGESTED READING

Valins. M. 1990. Growing Old in England. *Spectrum.* May: 20–23.

BEAUMONT, BRYN MAWR, PENNSYLVANIA

The 1912 Austin family music room, showpiece of the Beaumont facility, is dominated by a magnificent organ and an ornately gilded and painted ceiling, which was originally conceived by an Austrian artist and has been restored by Brian Cesario of nearby Philadelphia. (Architecture: Ann C. Capron; interiors: Arthur Shuster, Inc.; carpeting: Designweave, Charleston; wall fabric: Payne; throw pillow fabric: Scalamandre; tables: Century, IPF; lamps: Frederick Cooper; sofas: Drexel with Drexel fabric; chairs: Century with Scalamandre fabric; photo: Tom Crane.)

CHAPTER THREE

MARKET RESEARCH AND FEASIBILITY

BEAUMONT, BRYN MAWR, PENNSYLVANIA

The formal dining room, which had been the old mansion's main dining room, still has its original wood paneling. To adapt the room for seniors—cutting the glare yet allowing the recessed window shutters to remain operative—the designers specified tailored lace window panels. The scalloped valence was copied after the original one. (Architecture: Ann C. Capron; interiors: Arthur Shuster, Inc.; carpeting: Charleston; tables: Falcon; chairs: Shelby Williams with American Contract Textiles vinyl seats, Kravet fabric backs; valence fabric: Scalamandre; lace curtains: Naco; photo: Tom Crane.)

Marketing dominated the functional areas of business during the 1980s, and while it may not ride quite so high in the 1990s, marketing certainly will continue to be a most important functional area. Indeed, it can be argued that marketing is the primary activity of business, as it cuts across all other functions. Clearly, marketing is much more than the marketing department—it is the activity everyone in a company must be committed to in order for the company to succeed.

Traditionally speaking, marketing is the moving of goods from the point of production to the ultimate point of consumption. In the seniors housing industry, it is better to think in terms of moving the customer to the product, since the product is, by necessity, stationary. In the services domain, where production and consumption occur simultaneously, marketing may be thought of as an enabling or facilitating process, creating an environment conducive to the consumer's use of the service. In senior housing, developers are selling and marketing both a product (space and meals) and a service (the amenities or service packages offered by the retirement facility, as well as the medical and personal care services included in many retirement settings).

First and foremost, marketing is concerned with generating the business enterprise's revenue or sales—the top line. The other business functions, such as finance, architecture, design, construction, accounting, legal, operations, and human resources, are responsible for transforming the top line to the bottom line as effectively and as efficiently as possible, thereby maximizing profit over an extended time frame. Peter Drucker, the noted management philosopher, rethinks this construct of maximizing profit to one of *minimizing* profit with which to carry out the goals and objectives of the business enterprise. Drucker's test of a business's success is its survival from year to year and its ability to keep its customers. Cast in this light, management's task is to keep in balance all the forces that affect business for the long term, with marketing serving as a key business function in perpetuating the business enterprise by generating the top line, consistently fulfilling customer needs, and providing customer satisfaction.

Marketing is mentioned frequently (and sometimes synonymously) with sales. While sales is a component of marketing, marketing is nonetheless significantly more than sales. Marketing begins with market research to determine the market's needs, followed by the channeling of these needs into development, site selection, architecture, design, construction, and ultimately operations. Marketing also includes such elements as onsite merchandising, advertising, promotion, public relations, and pricing—and, yes, sales.

These charts track the progression of national demographic trends against those for a given market area. (Data courtesy of National Planing Data Corporation.)

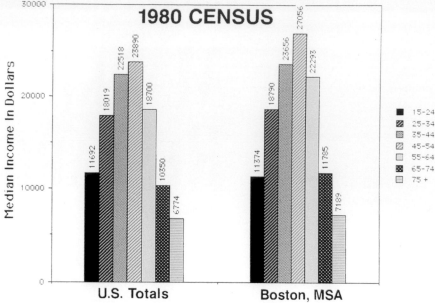

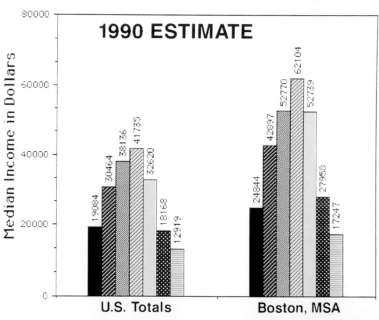

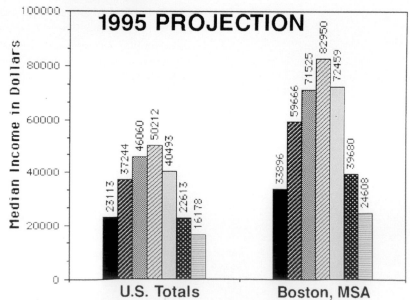

THE MARKET

In the planning, development, marketing, and administration of retirement housing, custom-tailored programs and structures to meet local market needs are critically important for the long-term success of a facility. What does the seniors market want? This is a fundamental question that needs to be answered objectively, without imposing the planner/developer's personal bias of what he or she *suspects* the older adult market wants. In the 1980s, there was tremendous reliance on mere speculation as to what seniors wanted in a development; sophisticated marketing research is now more prevalent.

A clear definition of a targeted and actual market can help make project realities match initial expectations. The paramount question is, *Who are we designing this project for?* Furthermore, what are the end users' expectations regarding the delivered product and services? And how can the design and management team's efforts be used to create a sense of value for the end users?

Variables in market preferences may be affected by region, physiological acuities, and the activity and educational levels of a prospective resident market. While stereotypes are not universally applicable to all individuals, a median model for a potential market must be established to design for minimally acceptable standards.

In a competitive market economy, the consumer is generally the driver. With increasing numbers of full-service senior facilities being developed, this truism is even more applicable. The seasoned owner/developer, banker, administrator, architect, or designer understands the role that preference plays in the decision-making process. Unfortunately, many decisions regarding seniors' preferences are made based on erroneous, outdated, or stereotypical models; to overcome this problem, a thorough, up-front study of a local market is invaluable. This involves face-to-face contact with market prospects in a comfortable nonthreatening exchange. A large number of prospects should be surveyed to ensure that a fair cross-section sampling has been obtained.

Any market research should start out free of bias. The historical approach to the seniors market has been cautious, with developers assuming wellness and health to be rarities existing within a sea of frailty. Such developers often have focused on what older individuals *cannot* do, rather that on what they *can*. Indeed, the general societal rationale is that after age 65, expectations of an individual's abilities (and, correspondingly, value) diminish. Past tendencies have also been to place senior consumers within classifications and categories, and then to assume that they will always react accordingly. Planners often forget that within each individual, there remains the persona that was present earlier in life.

MARKETING RESEARCH

Marketing research for retirement communities should ask two major questions: First, are there enough people in the specific market area to fill the facility in a reasonable amount of time (or, in more general terms, is there sufficient demand for the product?); and second, is the specific product to be developed the right product for the market? Within these two major foci, several other important considerations need to be addressed.

A significant distinction needs to be made between the need-driven and the demand-driven potential resident. To put it another way, what are the *push* or *pull* factors that encourage a senior to leave his or her home to live in a residential retirement facility? For instance, as one increases in age, the need for an alternative living environment may become a reality. Declining health, the loss of a spouse, or both, may lead the senior to be "pushed" from his or her home or apartment. This is a *need-driven* consideration. On the other hand, younger seniors, or those who are in good health, need to be enticed or "pulled" into the retirement living environment. This is a *demand-driven* consideration. To be sure, each of the decision factors plays a role in any given senior's decision to move, with each individual or couple placing a varying degree of weight on the two dimensions.

Traditional market-demand studies utilize census track data and measure the number of households in the primary market who are both income- and age-qualified. In the consumer market information industry, firms such as National Planning Data Corporation, CACI, and National Decision Systems, continuously update census data with sophisticated demographic analyses and forecasting models, which can be tailored to primary market areas. The primary market area is variously defined as existing within a 5-, 10-, 15-, or 25-mile radius from the site of the retirement facility. Additional sophisticated market-demand studies also look into travel time, distance, and access to the proposed site, rather than merely drawing concentric mileage circles around the proposed site to assess the market demand. A demographic chart of the age- and income-qualified households in the market area is analyzed, and a projected market penetration rate (the number of people, expressed as a percentage of the target market, that can be reasonably expected to use the product or service) of 1, 2, 3, 5, or 6 percent of such individuals is assumed. This analysis determines if the proposed facility size is appropriate for the estimated market demand.

For example, let us assume a conservative 3 percent penetration rate from 6,325 age- and income-qualified households living within a 10-mile radius of a proposed site. This would yield a market demand of 190 people. If there were no competing facilities of identical or similar offerings, we could assume that a 190-room single-occupancy facility would be market-feasible.

This quantitative study of market demand, when corrected for population changes, development, existing and potential competition, and other economic contingencies, yields a net pool of potential prospects within the primary market area. Determining this number after the assumption of market penetration yields the number of units required to satisfy present and near-future demand.

In addition to the demand analysis of the primary market area, a similar study of the secondary and tertiary market areas will determine the utility of adding more units to satisfy this potential

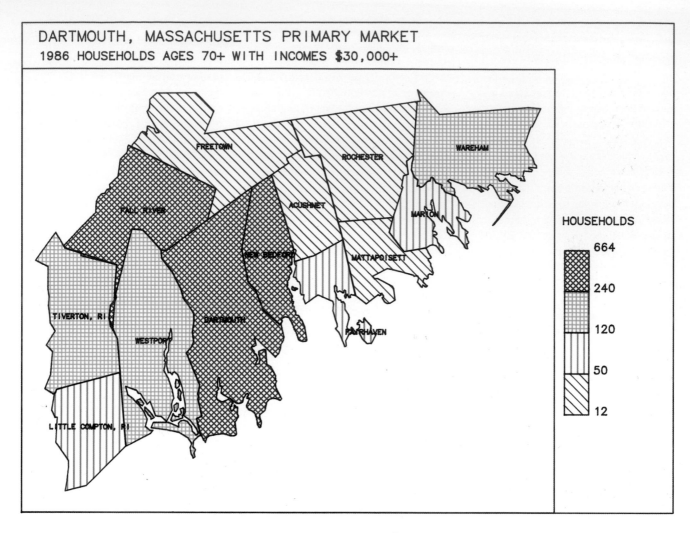

PRIMARY MARKET MAP

Density of age- and income-qualified households in a primary market area is tracked by town in this map. (Courtesy of Elder Care Services, Inc., and National Planning Data Corporation.)

additional demand. (For more information, The American Association of Homes for the Aging, in Washington, D.C., has published a booklet, *Market and Economic Feasibility Studies*, that addresses this subject in detail.)

This traditional demographic analysis requires a more discriminating look. For instance, in a case study cited by Brecht and Peters (1989), the authors discuss the number of renters, the gender of the residents, and the extended or multigenerational household as important data to tease out when making the "go/no go" decision. While the overall statistics in the case study suggested a "go" decision, a more careful look suggested the opposite—the number of renters was significantly higher than the norm, suggesting a propensity for staying in place by people who had already simplified their life-style. Also, the number of females was significantly lower than the average, suggesting that selling to the male and couples populations in this

demographic area would pose a greater difficulty. And the number of self-identified "others" was significantly higher than the norm, suggesting that the heads of households might be the patriarchs of large, multigenerational family structures—not a probable sale for retirement housing.

After obtaining a positive reading on a quantitative demographic market-demand study, the development team should design a mail survey questionnaire to assess the interest and attitudes toward the existence of retirement communities in the primary and secondary market areas. Some research firms use telephone survey methods. There are several mailing list companies that produce labels for seniors and will also segment age- and income-qualified individuals within certain zip codes. These mailing lists can be purchased, and the questionnaires printed and analyzed relatively inexpensively, especially when viewed in the context of the overall costs of developing and designing a retirement community. In addition to providing more data upon which to make a go/no-go decision on the development, the survey results can be used as supporting documentation to convince local planning or zoning boards that a significant demand exists for the retirement community, perhaps simplifying the zoning deliberations—planning or zoning boards are influenced by the responses of their own citizenry, and survey data are compelling forces in planning or zoning board meetings.

While a quantitative market-demand study and follow-up mail questionnaires are important, they should not be the only feasibility tests for continued development—they must first be supplemented with a qualitative study. The qualitative study, which is usually conducted in a focus-group setting, is designed to elicit in-depth responses and lengthy discussion on the local attitudes and dispositions regarding retirement housing in general, what type of housing is preferred, how much the market residents are willing to pay for the housing, and which elements from the array of available amenities are deemed most important. Deliberate selection of focus-

group participants can begin the pre-marketing phase of the development. Typically, potential focus-group participants are prescreened by telephone, and a prescreening document should be carefully prepared so as to maximize each participant's commitment to the focus-group session. The focus group serves two key purposes: to collect information for the planner, and to give back information from the planner to enlighten the neighborhood, the town, and its leaders. Focus-group members should include local business, religious, and political leaders (who have parents, grandparents, aunts, and uncles who are potential facility residents, as well as influence in the community and with planning and zoning boards), a cross-section of potential facility residents (prequalified by age and income), abutters (who might attempt to block the development, especially if they do not know what a retirement community really is), and a random sample of townspeople (who can "talk up" the project and have a feel for what the town might be most interested in).

Focus-group meetings should last no more than two hours and should be led by an experienced focus-group leader,

who, together with the development team, should prepare a series of questions to be answered by the group. Investors, planners, and other interested backers of the project often watch the focus group proceedings via a live closed-circuit hookup, and the meetings are videotaped for further review as well. It is best to set up group participants with people of similar backgrounds (some focus-group leaders prefer to segregate by gender), and several focus groups of 12 to 15 people each should meet in order to get a good representation of the issues and answers to the questions.

Focus-group participants should be treated extremely well. It is important to remember that the way in which the focus group is managed will strongly influence the group participants' expectations of the way in which the retirement facility will be managed. Each focus session should be catered, and breakfast, lunch or dinner should be served, if possible. At the very least, a well-presented selection of hors d'oeuvres or pastries with coffee, tea, and soft drinks should be offered. In addition, each participant should receive an incentive of $20 to $30 for participating. A memorable amenity,

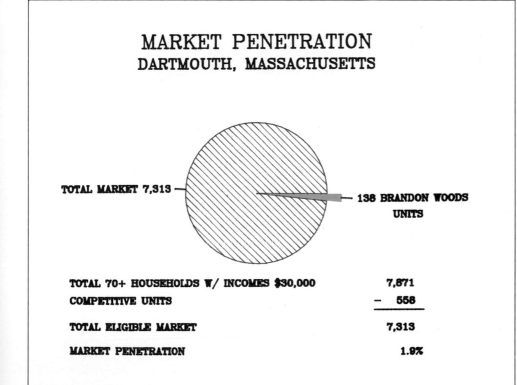

MARKET PENETRATION
DARTMOUTH, MASSACHUSETTS

TOTAL MARKET 7,313

138 BRANDON WOODS UNITS

TOTAL 70+ HOUSEHOLDS W/ INCOMES $30,000	7,871
COMPETITIVE UNITS	− 558
TOTAL ELIGIBLE MARKET	7,313
MARKET PENETRATION	1.9%

MARKET PENETRATION PIE CHART

A prospective facility's total units are shown as a percentage of the total available market. Typical market penetration rates are between 2 and 6 percent. (Courtesy of Elder Care Services, Inc., and National Planning Data Corporation.)

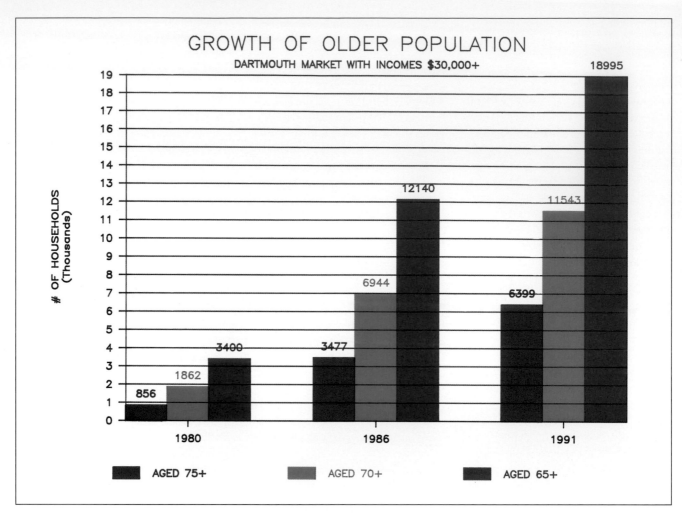

GROWTH OF OLDER POPULATION

DARTMOUTH MARKET WITH INCOMES $30,000+

18995

12140

11543

6944

6399

3400   3477

1862

856

 # OF HOUSEHOLDS (Thousands)

1980   1986   1991

■ AGED 75+   ■ AGED 70+   ■ AGED 65+

Charts like this one track demographic trends among age- and income-qualified households in given market areas. (Courtesy of Elder Care Services, Inc., and National Planning Data Corporation.)

such as an Express Mail or Federal Express package, can support the focus group session by confirming each person's participation. For many seniors, an express package simultaneously supports the importance of the focus group and of themselves.

After meeting with focus groups, a most sophisticated market analysis should then be conducted. Joyce Parr, director of the Foundation for Aging Research (FAR) has created a data set based on 2,500 households in four different types of American counties. FAR took a stratified random sample of senior-headed households which was balanced to represent the counties and their respective regions. The questionnaire segmented the respondent groups by age, income, functional health level, and location, and six fundamental determinants were researched: demographic and personal variables; interest variables; preferred location and design features; preferred services and contractual

arrangements, and type of sponsorship; reasons for considering a move, and concerns thereof; and reasons given by those not interested in moving to retirement housing for their hesitancy to make such a move. The FAR research method can be extended to test demographic variables for any market area, which can then be correlated to the FAR data base. For example, a five-mile radius around a specific site "can be compared for relative size of the market for a given type of project" (Parr 1990). FAR selects census tracts from the market area that would maximize the opportunity to reach the largest number of qualified respondents for a given facility. Random samples are then taken from the tracts, and any household, regardless of the age of its residents, has an equal chance to receive the FAR questionnaire—mailing lists are not used. This type of statistically valid sample, especially when augmented by the three types of marketing research already discussed, gives the developer the most accurate forecast possible. When FAR makes a recommendation to a developer they "specify the number of older people who are financially qualified, are likely to be interested in a specific kind of project in a specific location and who feel they will be ready to move within a two- to five-year period" (Parr, Green, and Behncke 1989). Additionally, FAR surveys the competition and competitive entry into the market. In addition to simplifying the go/no-go decision, positive results in each of the four research methods will better enable the developer to find project financing and to design the housing product for the specific market.

The two most important distinctions between people who are interested in moving to retirement housing and those who are not is the type of residence they now occupy and whether they have children living nearby. "Other variables which discriminate significantly between those who are interested in moving and those who are not are the types of activities in which people are currently involved and how limited they feel by their health. When variables like activities and health are held constant, age or living alone [are] not . . . significant discriminator[s]" (Parr 1990). The FAR research can also be used for determining preferences for design, service packages, and geographic location, and a marketing plan can be developed from these data. Other applications of this sort of research might include determining long-term insurance interest, desires of the single elderly, and the impact upon seniors of living more than 50 miles from their adult children.

MARKET SEGMENTS

Professionals in the study of aging have become most knowledgeable in segmenting the over-65 population. Yet many who are not involved in studying, working with, or designing products for seniors tend to lump all people over 65 into one group. Indeed, this is understandable, since almost all people upon reaching 65 begin collecting Social Security. Nonetheless, significant differences do exist among individuals over 65. One

popular and easily understood method of segmenting this population uses the basic subgroupings of *Go-gos*, *Slow-gos*, and *No-gos*.

PRIMARY RETIREMENT. The primary retirement market is known as the go-gos. Often newly retired from their principal vocations (although some may still be working), they are a very active group, with high expectations of future activity, including a second vocation or development of various avocations, including hobbies, volunteerism, education, or travel. This group is generally in good health.

Most primary retirees' children are no longer living at home, and their parents are often still living. Most own their own homes but are squeezed by the demands of children who may be in college, recently married, or looking to borrow a down payment on a first home. They may also have elderly parents in need of assistance. This group is often the most difficult to convince of a need for congregate housing for themselves, although they may be more receptive when the discussion turns to their parents. Their decision to move will be based on preference, not on need (which might not be the case for their parents). This group has the most diverse set of available options for senior housing.

Primary retirees' preferences are often driven by having more available time and convenience considerations. They are often trying to catch up on things long put off due to job- and family-related obligations. Many go-gos are affluent and mobile, enjoy traveling, dining in fine restaurants, and seeking high-quality entertainment, and see themselves as cashing in on their many years of productive work. These individuals have a sufficient income and savings to enjoy a life-style of carefree living. They look for a wide variety of goods and services to support their self-concept and their own personal feeling of having made it.

SECONDARY RETIREMENT. The secondary retirement market is nicknamed the slow-gos, is more affected by increasing acuity issues than are the go-gos. Secondary retirement demonstrates the broadest extremes of health—more and

more individuals in their mid-70s are still very alert and active, and many are far from being truly retired. Most are active in some type of volunteer work or family activities, and many are beginning second or third careers that often began as avocations.

Slow-gos' decisions regarding housing tend to be more need-driven. Most of these seniors find that issues of physical security, manageability of their residences, ready availability of health services, a modicum of conveniences, and a sense of community are important. Those who have lost a spouse, often feel a need for social activity and companionship, even if it is not intimate. Some of these retirees have ample time; therefore, time-saving conveniences are usually not among their priorities when making a decision to relocate. Indeed, some of them may find the latest technology and conveniences frightening or confusing.

Most secondary retirees own or have owned their own homes, and three out of four have their mortgages paid off, giving them a fair amount of collateral and debt-free assets. This group is probably the most affluent of the three retiree market segments, although their assets are not always liquid. Of course, specific income-qualification information must be verified by demographic data in the target market area.

Because of this group's diversity in health needs and activity levels, there is a wide range of available housing options, including independent housing units, assisted living units, and skilled nursing units, depending on need. This diversity contributes to this market segment being the most challenging to pinpoint in terms of preferences regarding service packages and housing needs. A delicate balance of emphasis between life-style- and security-oriented elements is most often desirable.

The slow-gos, while still active, have begun to slow down a bit. They are, for the most part, healthy but with declining mobility, and still engage in many of the activities they took part in when they were go-gos. However, they may not be as active with the same level of frequency or with the same endurance as when they were go-gos.

TERTIARY RETIREMENT. This group is generally categorized by older retirees faced with declining health and income status. Often referred to as the no-gos, a large percentage (but by no means all) of this group is driven by absolute needs of assistance in health care and the tasks of daily living. This group therefore has the fewest residential living options. Time-saving conveniences are usually of little significance to tertiary retirees, since they, like the secondary retirees, usually have ample available time.

Depending on health conditions, tertiary retirees or their family members tend to choose residence in several types of housing: independent living; assisted living; personal care; skilled nursing; or specialty units, such as Alzheimer's units. Usually the most difficult aspect of life to these retirees is the finality of most decisions made at this phase of life. Due to decreased mobility, this group needs a greater array of mental, social, physical, and spiritual stimuli from the outside. The challenge to increase the dignity of daily living exists more for this group than for any other segment of society.

No-gos' health tends to have declined significantly, and their mobility is usually severely limited. While some may be able to maintain themselves in the activities of daily living, most will soon be needing long-term care or other forms of assistance, such as meals on wheels, handicapped transportation services, home health care, and so forth. The oldest of the three retiree segments, these individuals may also find themselves with reduced income and savings with which to meet their needs.

VIEWS OF AGING

The concept of "senior living" as a valid life-style, independent of extended family, is still a relatively new concept to American society. At most, the concept is 20 to 30 years old, and is still evolving. As different generations age, the factors on which they will base decisions will relate to the circumstances to which they were accustomed during their "prime" years of life. Understandably, then, we can expect each succeeding generation's view of meaningful retirement living to change. In fact, today's seniors abhor the very word *retirement*—they ask, "Who's retiring from life?" More and more, we are coming to view life as a continuum of activities that need not occur in any prescribed order. For instance, the view of a woman's child-bearing years is markedly different today from what it was in the 1950s, and we can expect this and similar issues to affect each generation's outlook on retirement. In the future, it is likely that education, socialization, recreation, acquisition of material belongings, vocations, and avocations will increasingly become interspersed in miniphases of life, rather than taking place in the traditional sequence of educational, child-bearing and -rearing, vocational, and retirement/recreational phases.

Despite these changing views of aging, survey data can tell us certain things about the seniors market as it exists today. For example, approximately 40 percent of those over 49 years of age have a fair amount of disposable income and are in good health. These individuals, often referred to as *actively affluent*, are roughly 60 percent men. Most are under age 65 with no children at home. These individuals are prime candidates for travel, financial planning, beauty products, and health and wellness products.

Approximately 22 percent of those over 49 are married women with living spouses; twenty-five percent are widowed. Key marketing issues to this group are financial and health products and services. The balance of the female population over age 50 is below the poverty level, with many segmented as "ill" or "disadvantaged."

Of the entire retired seniors population, 15 percent are over 50 years of age, still have good health, and are above the poverty level. Out of every five such individuals, four are men who were primary wage-earners before retiring. Many of these individuals, although retired, want to stay in the mainstream of social contact, rather than isolating themselves.

What do these sorts of market-segmentation and consumer-preference data have to do with the nuts and bolts of facility development and administration? Each market segment contains latitude for individual tastes and preferences. Using profiles of market segments, base assumptions can be made as points of departure when planning a project.

For example, for the primary retiree with a very active life-style, time-saving conveniences that simplify tasks of daily living are usually important. This go-go is familiar with most of the gadgets that make life easier: microwave ovens, dishwashers, trash compactors, cellular telephones, personal computers, answering machines, voice mail, security alarms, garage door openers, automatic coffee brewers, central vacuum systems, instant bank teller machines, and so on.

All of these inventions save time, which can then be used elsewhere for other interests and pursuits. To a young retiree who has grown up with these conveniences, learning to use them is perceived as being within any normal person's ability and grasp. Conversely, trying to sell these same features to an older individual of age 80 may not be fruitful. To a secondary retiree of advanced age, time savings or convenience issues may have little relevance in their life-style and therefore be of marginal interest. To most seniors of this age, meaningful use of an abundance of time is usually the challenge, not the creation of *more* spare time.

PSYCHOGRAPHICS

Another segmentation approach, taken by Jim Gollub from SRI International in a study sponsored by the National Association for Senior Living Industries, is the use of *psychographic profiles*—in essence, disregarding age as a discriminator and using psychology, socioeconomics, and health as the keys to understanding how older adults want to live. The study, called *LAVOA* (for *Lifestyles and Values of Older Adults*), was designed to enable organizations that provide products and services for seniors to have a better understanding of how older adults think and how they differ from one another. SRI identified six distinct older adult consumer segments: attainer, adapter, explorer, pragmatist, martyr, and preserver (Gollub 1989).

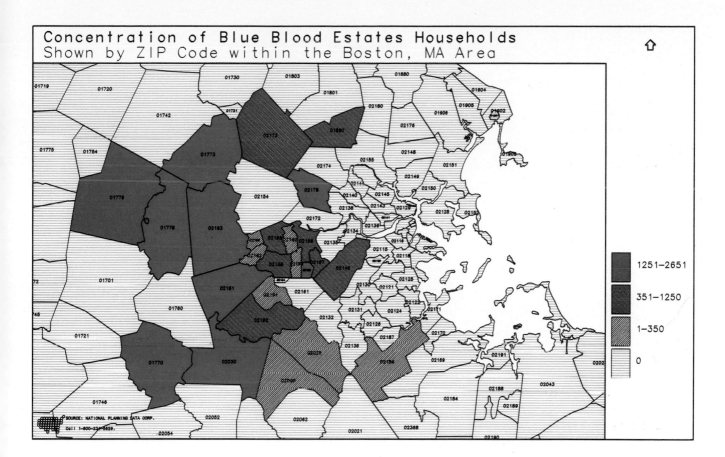

Concentration of Blue Blood Estates Households
Shown by ZIP Code within the Boston, MA Area

■	1251–2651
▨	351–1250
▧	1–350
□	0

SOURCE: NATIONAL PLANNING DATA CORP.
Call 1-800-234-5429.

While the LAVOA segments are valuable for organizations designing products or services that cut across all segments of society, caution should be used when attempting to extrapolate these data to a specific market. The LAVOA segments are arranged according to four personality scales:

1. *Autonomy–dependence:* the need to be on one's own
2. *Extroversion–introversion:* the degree to which people are outer-directed and seek social involvement
3. *Self-indulgence–self-denial:* the extent to which people seek gratification
4. *Openness to change–resistance to change:* the extent to which people are adaptable

This type of analysis reinforces the point that not all seniors should be grouped in the same category.

REFERENCES

Brecht, S., and Peters, H. 1989. Household Clues to Solve the Mystery of Market Potential. *Retirement Housing Report.* October.

Gollub, J., and Javits, H. 1989. Six Ways to Age. *American Demographics.* June: 28.

Parr, J. 1990. How to Get a Fix on Service-Oriented Senior Housing. The Foundation for Aging Research Prototypical Data Set, prepared for the seminar session for the National Association of Home Builders Annual Convention.

Parr, J., Green, S., and Behncke, C. 1989. *Lifestyles and Housing of Older Adults.* New York: The Haworth Press, Inc.

Wolfe, D. 1990. *Serving the Ageless Market.* New York: McGraw-Hill.

SUGGESTED READINGS

Menchin, R. 1989. *The Mature Market.* Chicago: Probus Publishing Company.

Moore, J. 1988. Misconceptions About the Elderly. *Commercial Investment Real Estate Journal.* January/February: 24–25.

Meister, S., and Kitchen, J. 1988. Marketing Lessons from CCRC Residents. *Retirement Housing Report.* Volume 2, Number 12.

Winklevoss, H., and Powell, A. 1984. *Continuing Care Retirement Communities: An Empirical, Financial, and Legal Analysis.* Homewood, Ill.: Richard D. Irwin, Inc.

PSYCHOGRAPHIC MARKET MAP

Household density for a particular psychographic group—"Blue blood estates" in this case—is tracked here by zip code. Blue blood estates are among America's wealthiest upper strata, but similar maps can be prepared for other socioeconomic types. (Courtesy National Planning Data Corporation.)

CHAPTER FOUR

MARKETING PLANNING, STRATEGY, AND IMPLEMENTATION

SURREY PLACE, CHESTERFIELD, MISSOURI

In the dining room, the design team specified armchairs and side chairs, since some residents need arm supports, while others find it easier to slide in and out sideways. Vinyl-coated chintz chair upholstery has a lattice pattern that complements the carpet. Across the corridor, large windows and glass doors overlook the courtyard. (Architecture: The Wischmeyer Architects; interiors: LVK Associates; tables: Berco; chairs: American of Martinsville with Lazarus Contract fabric; carpet: Harbinger; chandeliers: Gross Chandelier Co.; photo: Alise O'Brien.)

THE MARKETING PLANNING PROCESS

The first step in bringing marketing research and feasibility into action is to design a marketing plan. A marketing plan can be compared to a pilot's flight plan—the pilot knows where he or she wants to go and needs to design a flight plan that will lead there. The pilot assesses the weather, the flight equipment and instruments, the capabilities of the specific aircraft, and so on, all in an effort to plot the most efficient course for reaching the intended destination safely.

While creating the marketing plan for a retirement facility, the marketing director will search for the best route for the facility to take in order to arrive at the desired market position. Just as the pilot assesses the weather, the marketing director assesses the economic environment; as the pilot plots navigation points, the marketing director aims for target quotas. The key is constant attention on effectiveness and efficiency, which will result in targeted profit for the operation.

Specifically, the marketing plan is a document describing the precise and systematic approach that the marketing group should take to market and sell the property and its services. There are several steps in the marketing planning process. The *executive summary* is for quick review by management and presents the purpose and primary goals of the marketing plan followed by a table of contents. The key is to identify the nature, scope, and variety of the targeted market audience(s) to which the marketing effort will be directed for each of the products being offered by the residential community. Each market segment, along with the intended approach to reach and penetrate it, must be specified. How each market segment will contribute to the whole must also be addressed.

The *situation analysis* addresses the background data on the market, the

---

Portions of this chapter are made possible by the generous contribution of the National Association of Home Builder's publication Senior Housing Marketing Specialist for the Older Retirement Market *written by Barbara Kleger, President of Senior Living Associates of Media, Pennsylvania and Skip Kedney, President of Kedney and Associates of Boca Raton, Florida. The authors wish to express their sincere thanks for the rights to extract information from this publication.*

product, the competition, and the business and economic environment. Significant external and internal factors, including demographic, economic, technological, political/legal, and social/cultural issues, may affect the feasibility of the plan, and all these should be assessed and accounted for. In addition, the current market situation should be addressed, with specific regard to size, growth, the specific needs of each market segment, the market's perceptions of the operation's product(s), and its buying behavior. In analyzing the products, total sales, unit prices, and amenities, the situation analysis should delineate the contribution margin and net profit for each product. In addition, the competition needs to be assessed, including its size, goals, market share, quality, marketing strategies, and other competitive factors. Lookalike competition is not the only type that should be analyzed—indeed, apartment or condominium housing projects, for example, may compete very effectively with a retirement community, especially in terms of price.

The *opportunities and threats* section of the marketing planning process lists the key opportunities and fundamental obstacles (external factors), as well as the strengths and weaknesses (internal factors) working for and against an effective marketing effort. The opportunities and threats should be ranked in order of priority and lead to the setting of objectives, strategies, and tactics.

Objectives detail specific targeted results in terms of sales volume or number of units sold, market share, and profit, and are divided into financial objectives and marketing objectives. Financial objectives state both the short-term (less than one year) and long-term (usually one to five years) rate of return desired by the owners, which are then converted into marketing objectives. For example, if an organization wants to obtain a certain sales volume, that volume must be translated into a certain number of units sold per week or per month. In addition to sales volume, the plan should specify how many contacts should be made by phone or by mail during a given time period, how many appointments need to be scheduled, how many public relations events should be staged, and how many social events will be held.

Objectives must be quantifiable within specific time frames, should be stated and structured to flow in logical order from one to the next, and should be sufficiently challenging (to produce maximum effort) yet attainable.

Marketing strategies, the approaches that will be taken to reach the stated objectives, consist of broad decisions on target markets, marketing positioning and mix, and marketing expenditure levels. Various strategies may yield certain objectives. For example, if a particular sales volume is the objective, this can be attained either by selling more units at lower selling prices or by increasing the selling price and selling fewer units. Strategy is formulated by choosing which approach to take.

The *action plan* answers the questions of what will be done, who will do it, when will it be done, and how much will it cost. This is the detailed step-by-step action that will be taken to implement the strategy statement, a written document that becomes the marketing group's "to do" list, complete with correct sequencing and resource allocation.

Budget and resource allocation summarizes the financial results of the plan and should be broken down into the costs for each step in the action plan as well as for other areas (such as human resources and outside contracts). In concert with finance, marketing should develop an income statement listing revenues and expenses (both fixed and variable), which should illustrate the project's

FORWOOD MANOR, WILMINGTON, DELAWARE

The library has comfortable wing chairs where residents can settle and read for long periods. French doors open to the inner corridor that encircles the public areas. (Architecture: Moeckel Carbonell Associates; interiors: Interior Design Associates; table, chairs: Madison Square; bookcase: Council Craftsman; wing chairs: Southwood; lamps: Hallmark; wallcovering: Koroseal Wallcovering; draperies: Brunschwig & Fils, fabricated by Fantagraph; photo: Tom Crane.)

MARKETING STRATEGY FOR REGENCY PARK RETIREMENT VILLAGE

TARGET MARKET

Households with $25,000+ annual income, with emphasis on females over 75 years of age.

POSITIONING

The most luxurious retirement community with the widest range of services within a 25-mile radius.

PRODUCT LINE

One- and two-bedroom senior residential units for purchase or rental.

PRICE

On average, 15% above lookalike competition.

SALES FORCE

One marketing director and six full-time retirement counselors for first 30 months of opening; reduce to one marketing director and two full-time retirement counselors when retirement community is 95% occupied and stabilized.

SERVICES

Full-service dining, including private dining for residents' private entertainment; medical services and long-term care facility on site; weekly housekeeping and flat linen; wide range of educational, social, and travel programs; complimentary limousine and convenience store on premises; separate beauty and barber salons; library; chapel; meeting, craft, gardening, and workshop rooms; full maintenance and repair service; 24-hour guarded security at community entrance and 24-hour on-premises security, including video monitoring.

ADVERTISING

Will be directed at the target market and support the positioning strategy, with emphasis on luxury and simultaneous leisure and socially beneficial activities programming; advertising and promotions budget to be gradually decreased as community becomes fully absorbed.

PROMOTION

Target three local newspapers per month for promotion coverage during the first 30 months from opening; decrease to one promotion event per month after full absorption.

RESEARCH AND DEVELOPMENT

Monitor residents using valid statistical sampling to determine if service levels are needed and being delivered.

MARKETING RESEARCH

Monitor competition, both existing facilities and subsequent new entries; assess service and residential product as data for expansion into other market areas.

This simple marketing scheme shows the wide range of factors that must be anticipated and accounted for when planning to develop a retirement facility.

---

profitability. The most effective plans do not skimp on the marketing budget—a well-orchestrated, fully professional, campaign is critical to the success of the development. For most retirement communities, $4,000 to $8,000 per unit should be budgeted.

Finally, the *control and measurement* step describes how the plan will be monitored, how and when the results will be reviewed, measured, and analyzed, and what actions or contingency plans should be implemented if the stated objectives and end results are not being met.

At the conclusion of this marketing planning process, the plan should be submitted to appropriate management levels for approval. The contents of the plan should not come as a surprise to anyone required to approve it—the development of the plan should entail the frequent and consistent consultation of executive management. Indeed, the final marketing plan should be a negotiated agreement with marketing and executive management, developed during the marketing planning process.

PREMARKETING

Premarketing takes place before the retirement center has all proper zoning clearances and perhaps long before financing is in place. Indeed, premarketing may be simultaneous to the feasibility study and test-marketing phases of the development process. In short, premarketing is a preliminary testing of the waters that takes place prior to the commitment of significant amounts of marketing capital.

Focus groups, in addition to their market feasibility utility, can be used as a premarketing vehicle. Group participants should include prospective residents as well as key leaders in the community—religious leaders, local government leaders, volunteer organization leaders, and so forth. If the proposed retirement center is far enough along in the development process, the focus group session can be held on the premises in a model unit or in the center's great room, dining room, or activities room. If the setting is exquisitely catered and consistent with the style of service to be offered—and it should be—the focus group participants will be left with a positive impression, which is the most important aspect of effective premarketing. The focus groups will also serve as good models for the formation of advisory boards, which should also be established and should be composed of a similar mix of participants.

Postal questionnaires can be used to inform the target market about the prospective retirement center and collect information regarding specific needs of the future residents. Questionnaires should include postage-paid response cards or make prominent mention of a toll-free response phone number, allowing prospective residents to respond while simultaneously giving the marketing staff a way to develop a list of interested potential residents (called prospects).

Seminars and lectures, either public or by invitation only, should be held to further inform members of the community about retirement living and the proposed development. Seminars, which can be used to address a wide range of subjects and can be cosponsored with local seniors organizations and businesses, are effective at communicating specific information in an atmosphere free of the pressure that might be construed in a one-on-one meeting between a sales staffer and a prospective resident. In addition, seminars can build excitement and interest in the project and attract valuable publicity.

Social gatherings—teas, tours, openings, ground-breakings and so forth—can also serve as effective premarketing activities. These events, which frequently may be hosted by the retirement center but *planned* by a local group of seniors, initiate a feeling of community and life-style long before the development is to become a reality.

ADVERTISING AND PROMOTION

While *advertising* and *promotion* typically refer to the line item in the controllable expenses column of an income statement, the terms *marketing communications mix* and *promotion mix* better describe our purposes here. Kotler (1988) introduces

the four categories, originally developed by the American Marketing Association in 1960, within the promotion mix:

- *Advertising* refers to any paid form of nonpersonal presentation and promotion of ideas, goods, or services by a defined sponsor (e.g., a television ad displaying the advantages of Tide soap over another soap/detergent product, a bordered section of a newspaper introducing a new physician to an established medical practice, etc.).
- *Sales promotion* is a short-term incentive to encourage purchase or sale of a product or service (e.g., a coupon that, when used with the purchase of an airline ticket, allows the purchaser of the airline ticket an automatic upgrade to first class).
- *Publicity* is nonpersonal stimulation of demand for a product, service, or business unit by planting commercially significant news about it in a published medium or obtaining favorable presentation on radio, television, or stage that is *not* paid for by the sponsor (e.g., an article published in a local newspaper discussing the benefit that a new retirement facility will bring to the community).
- *Personal selling* is an oral presentation in a conversation with one or more prospective purchasers for the purpose of making sales (e.g., a personal conversation between a retirement village representative and a senior citizen who may be a prospective resident in the retirement housing village).

We shall now examine each of these elements in greater detail.

ADVERTISING. The purpose of advertising retirement communities is to educate or inform the market about the product with the objective of building primary demand. In some regions of the United States, many people do not know what a modern, upscale retirement housing project looks like. The primary market may have no concept of a retirement project other than an image of a nursing or convalescent home. For retirement communities, therefore, the specific purpose of advertising is to counter this

image and attract age- and income-qualified prospects or their close family members by persuading them to visit the model unit or at the very least call for more information so that the developer/owner can create a prospect list.

Advertising may also be used to "remind" the market members that they may need senior housing in the future. As assisted living facilities are added to independent living communities (addressing the aging-in-place phenomenon), advertising needs to be directed to the children of the older adult market as well as to the older adults themselves. Indeed, older adults do not make impulse buying decisions to move into congregate settings—research suggests that older adults take considerable time in making these decisions. In a 1986 survey (Meister and Kitchen 1988), almost 40 percent of American retirement facility residents reported that they took four years from initial contact to actually moving into the community; 20 percent took between two to three years, almost 25 percent took between one to two years, and less than 20 percent made the decision to move during the first year after initial contact. With these statistics in mind, targeting the potential residents' children, who can influence the parents' decisions, becomes crucial.

In order to plan retirement housing advertising, the specific advertising objectives must be set and coordinated within the total promotion mix, and the target(s) to whom the advertising is to be directed must be clearly defined. For instance, if research in a particular market area for a congregate living environment identifies a significant number of 75-year-old, white, upper-middle-income women, the advertising should be directed toward them and to their children (as well as to their grandchildren, nieces, nephews, and so forth). Specifically, the advertisements should display people in their early 60s, since most seniors see themselves as some 10 to 15 years younger than they are.

Advertising may be displayed in various media, including direct mail, brochures or circulars, newspapers, magazines, radio, television, posters, signs, billboards, phone directories, and such novelties as matchbooks, calendars, pens, or pencils. Most experts agree that direct mail is the most effective method, generating an average effective response rate of 1 to 2 percent.

Any other form of media advertising should be coordinated with the direct mail programs. Major metropolitan newspapers generate better responses than small local papers, but the high costs require the marketing director to monitor the response rate closely. If this route is taken, ads should be placed in the family/home/living or magazine sections of the paper. Marketing directors should monitor the success of specific ads—do they generate leads? If not, change them quickly!

Ad copy should be printed in particularly large type and if a mail-in response is requested, the tear-off portion should provide large spaces to write in, as many older adults are no longer adept at writing neatly. The tear-off portion

should be located on the lowest outer edged portion of the ad, and the ad itself should be placed at the lower, outer edge of the page, preferably on a right-hand page.

When considering advertising in periodicals or on radio or television, careful analysis should be made to determine if the high costs are worth the results. If the sole criterion for success is lead generation, then the results of the ads can be easily assessed and the cost per generated lead can be calculated. Other factors also come into play. For instance, when advertising in a periodical with extensive use of color, color should also be used in the retirement community's ad. If advertising independent living, splashy colors may be used; for advertising assisted living, more subdued colors are called for.

The American Association of Retired Persons (AARP) gives the following

suggestions on how to communicate to older adults, which it uses to guide advertisers in its periodical, *Modern Maturity*:

1. *Begin a new lifetime.* Show older adults as open-minded and interested in acquiring new information. They want to be part of the world around them, not bypassed by it.
2. *Mix well.* Intergenerational and intercultural gatherings suggest that engaging new ideas and people reinforce the older adult's existence as being part of the world, not separated from it.
3. *Sampling creates loyalty.* People over 50 are experienced consumers and consider purchases, especially large purchases, very carefully. They read refund policies, warranties, and guarantees assiduously. Disclose everything about your product or service;

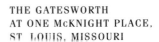

THE GATESWORTH
AT ONE McKNIGHT PLACE,
ST. LOUIS, MISSOURI

A postmodern portico enhances the sense of arrival. The broken arch—an architectural flourish repeated over the windows of the facade—is used as the center's logo. (Architecture: Arthur J. Sitzwohl & Associates; interiors: LVK Associates; photo: Barbara Eliott Martin.)

do not be afraid to give details—don't make a long story short. Coupons, trial periods, and other methods allowing them to sample the product or service creates loyalty.

4. *Simplify the complex.* Help them solve problems and coach them on how to cope with difficult situations and conditions. Experience has taught older adults how to recognize displeasure, dissatisfaction, and distress; be realistic and optimistic. Show older adults handling and solving problems, not caving in under stress. Demonstrate that your product or service can help them, and be specific.

5. *Show age in how they feel—not chronologically.* Most older adults see themselves as 10 to 15 years younger than they are, so take off at least 15 years when you advertise. Speak to the person, not his or her age.

6. *Don't worry, be happy.* Display seniors as being happy with their free time or actively engaged in volunteer work. Some want to relax in a hammock and enjoy the fruits of their labor, and others look forward to doing things they never had time to do.

7. *Feature sumptuous food and give high priority to entertaining.* Show older adults with groups, not alone. They still love the good food they enjoyed as youths, and many seniors can take a little more liberty on the "bad" food that tastes so good, so don't put them all on a diet.

8. *Keep it light.* A sense of humor goes a long way. With reduced life pressures, many older adults are not as serious as they once were. Pictures with smiling children and especially grandchildren send a particularly positive message.

9. *Romance the setting.* Seniors want to look and feel as attractive as ever. With more time for relationships, they extend their "dating" behavior with their spouses, significant others, and just others. Sex and candlelight dinners are *not* things of the past.

10. *Expand horizons.* Many adventures are waiting to be experienced. Many older adults have the means (time and money) to enjoy educational travel, lectures, workshops, and so forth—indeed, to be all they ever wanted to be.

SALES PROMOTION AND PUBLICITY. Promotion and publicity efforts should be preceded by a clear statement of both the long- and short-term objectives to be achieved. A key element to keep in mind when formulating these objectives is the concept of *creating* news rather than having someone react to an unplanned event. In essence, promotion and publicity should have the same objectives as advertising—generating qualified leads.

Although promotion and publicity usually rate behind advertising when selling consumer products and behind personal selling when marketing consumer products and manufactured goods, they rank equal to advertising in the promotion mix for retirement communities. While advertising may be perceived as "paid space" (which, of course, it is), promotion and publicity may be perceived with more credulity, since the public knows that they have not been bought.

Publicity and promotion are part of a larger concept—public relations—which is a critically important factor in senior living. Promotion and publicity are specialized forms of communication and involve the mastery and coordination of a variety of media vehicles. The ongoing processes of building a positive image for the retirement project in the minds of the community (and especially to the primary targeted market, their children, and referral networks) should be used as a vehicle to shape the image of the project as an authentic product for its intended purpose.

Both management and marketing staff should be available to community groups for making presentations on seniors-oriented issues. Targeted groups should include social, civic and professional organizations, and educational and philanthropic organizations. Management members should look for opportunities to be quoted in publications that are well-regarded by the primary market segment, which can promote the positive image desired by the facility.

It is critically important to follow up the qualified leads generated by promotions and publicity events so that they can be converted to prospects. If this work is not executed thoroughly and promptly, all the thoughtful advance work will be wasted.

PERSONAL SELLING

In the senior residential industry, individuals engaged in selling are variously referred to as retirement counselors, marketing representatives, sales representatives or consultants, account executives, salespeople, and so forth, and these titles will all be used in the following discussion. Some of the terms are attempts to mask the sales function, a response to the stereotypes many Americans have about the term *salesman*.

THE GATESWORTH AT ONE McKNIGHT PLACE, ST. LOUIS, MISSOURI

Stylized architectural-style detailing is painted on the 17-foot (5-meter) vertical space between the topmost gallery of the atrium and the skylight. (Architecture: Arthur J. Sitzwohl & Associates; interiors: LVK Associates; lounge chairs: Jack Cartwright with fabric by Ward Bennett for Brickel; tables: Intrex; lamps: Frederick Cooper; carpet: Design Weave; marble tile: Marble Technics; bench: Southwood Reproductions with fabric by DesignTex; trompe l'oeil: Ann Sheehan, LVK Associates designer; photo: Barbara Eliott Martin.)

Given the wide range of types of selling that various industries employ, it is important to distinguish those selling in the residential retirement market. Salespeople in this industry are involved in a hybrid function—on the one hand, they are selling a *product*, a place for public gatherings and for private residence, with walls, floors, ceilings, fixtures, and so forth; on the other hand, they are selling *life-style* and, in most settings, continued healthcare. While this life-style claim can be made about many products and services and the people who sell and deliver them, the overriding responsibility for sales individuals in the retirement facility industry is to communicate the intangible, to prospective residents and their families, to convey such notions as independence, freedom, convenience, comfort, companionship, longevity, safety, and peace of mind. Most prospective residents are moving from larger spaces to smaller ones, which can be easily perceived as a step down. When this reality is coupled with the perception of institutionalization, the task for the sales staff is unmistakably difficult.

While advertising, promotion, and publicity are all designed to project a positive image of the retirement community, the sales representative is the embodiment of the company. The salesperson is typically the first company-related person the potential resident will meet, and indeed, after a resident moves in, the person who sold the residence may become the resident's closest friend from among the entire retirement community staff. In this context, the term *retirement counselor* takes on real meaning—it is not just intended to mask the sales function. The salesperson may know many intimate details about the resident, and just as important, the resident knows that the salesperson knows.

Even before a prospective resident is taken on a tour of the facility, the sales representative should *qualify* the prospect. Qualifying a lead entails more than just determining the financial capability of the prospective resident—it means finding the person's preferred climate, desired proximity to friends or relatives, preference for the city, suburbs, or country, recreational interests, reasons and anticipated time frame for moving, and

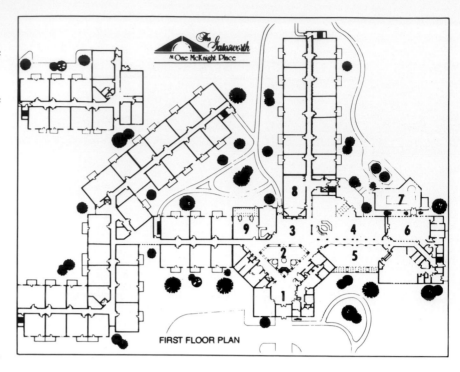

FIRST FLOOR PLAN

so on. These factors must be addressed in order for the representative to sell based on the prospect's need.

In order to sell affordability, the following rules of thumb may be helpful. The U.S. Bureau of Labor Statistics's elderly family budget (Rohrer and Bibb 1986) indicates that

retired householders can afford to pay no more than 61% of their disposable income on congregate fees. Thus . . . a married couple occupying a unit priced at $1,000 per month plus a $250 double-occupancy charge would require a before-tax annual income of $31,500. A widow would need an annual income of $24,500 to live in this unit. To occupy a CCRC unit priced at $2,000 per month, a widow and a married couple would require before-tax incomes of, respectively, $51,800 and $61,000 per year.

While the most effective form of advertising for senior living communities may be direct mail, the most effective (perhaps the *only* effective) form of *selling* retirement living is through personal contact. When selling, the retirement counselor presents the product and the services package, emphasizing the

health-care component when appropriate, overcomes objections, and when all goes well, closes the sale. While salespeople may find it easiest to focus only on selling it is most important for the sales staff in the retirement living industry to follow through by paying attention to resident satisfaction. Word of mouth is one of the more effective means for generating new leads and prospects, and a retirement counselor who follows through with a prospect-turned-resident can continue to generate leads and prospects who may have increasingly higher propensities to move toward the close—after all, their friends are already there! With this in mind, marketing representatives should try to arrange meetings of prospective and existing residents to begin the socialization process.

Given the high cost of developing, marketing, and operating a retirement center, the sales staff should be aware of how their sales efforts are converted to profitability. The practical need for this understanding can be demonstrated by examining the concept of *absorption*, the term used to express the net average measure of how many units in a retirement center are occupied in a month during the lease-up period (*net* takes into consideration the number of people who, for one reason or another, choose to move out once they have already moved in).

THE GATESWORTH AT ONE McKNIGHT PLACE, ST. LOUIS, MISSOURI

LEFT: First-level floor plan. Legend: 1. Entry and lobby. 2. Atrium. 3. Lounge. 4. Garden dining. 5. Colonnade room. 6. Fitness center. 7. Indoor pool and spa. 8. Theater/chapel. 9. Crafts room. (Architecture: Arthur J. Sitzwohl & Associates.)

RIGHT: A painted-wood trellis over the bar area looks like a gazebo and heightens the gardenlike effect. Residents can linger over drinks on one side of the cocktail bar; the other serves as a wait station. A painted-glass insert at the back of the bar screens the activities of the wait staff from view of bar patrons. (Architecture: Arthur J. Sitzwohl & Associates; interiors: LVK Associates; dining chairs: Chairmasters; loveseats: Brown Jordan; tables: Berco; upholstery: Duralee, DesignTex; carpet: Design Weave; wallcovering: Vicrtex, Schumacher & Co.; ceiling: Armstrong; photo: Alise O'Brien.)

In the formal Colonnade Room, ceiling beams detailed with traditional moldings are made of fiberglass. Other luxurious appointments include a mahogany armoire, bronze light fixtures, and stained-glass door panels. (Architecture: Arthur J. Sitzwohl & Associates; interiors: LVK Associates; seating: Council Craftsmen with fabric by DesignTex; tables: Chairmasters; carpet: Design Weave; chandeliers, sconces: Gross Chandelier; stained glass: custom-designed by LVK and made by Art Glass Unlimited; wallcovering: Carnegie Xorel, Schumacher & Co.; photo: Alise O'Brien.)

The absorption rate may determine a project's feasibility, regardless of the indications of feasibility studies, market research, demographics, and so on. In absolute numbers, a competitive retirement housing project located in a good market area will achieve a net fill rate of only four to six units per month. If the feasibility study assumes a faster net fill rate, the development is apt to have inadequate cash flow at the onset and will fold (or be sold for a fraction of its cost) before it ever gets started. Assuming that a hypothetical developer/owner estimates a net average fill rate of five units per month for a 150-unit rental retirement housing village with an average monthly rent of $1,500 per unit, the time to fill up at 100 percent occupancy would be 30 months, with a yield of $4,995,000 in rental revenue at the

30-month point. But if the facility averaged four leased units per month, instead of five, and if we assume a stabilized occupancy of 96 percent or 144 units, it would take 36 months to "fill" the facility. If the average net fill rate of five units per month were achieved, the developer would appreciate $2,205,000 more in revenue at the 36-month point than in the four-units-per-month instance, with corresponding drops in monthly revenue. And these revenue calculations do not even take into consideration operational and occupational overhead costs that begin accruing the moment the first occupant moves in. The revenue gap shown in this example demonstrates the importance of selling at a consistently high rate—even a small dropoff can make the difference between a facility succeeding or folding.

Specific strategies to move an older adult to close include cost of living comparisons, affordability descriptions, and addressing the financing options (equity conversions, reverse annuity mortgages, sale/lease-back, and so forth). Many people do not know how much they spend on the various services they enjoy, so all basic costs, extra charges, and planned or capped increases for fees and other charges should be clearly explained. A sales representative can walk a prospect through a cost of living comparison using the guidelines in the AARP's *Your Home, Your Choice*, and a financial worksheet can be drawn up listing all income and all monthly expenses, with the sales representative then isolating those expenses that would no longer be incurred separately but would be included in the costs of living in the retirement home.

Good reasons to move that the sales representative may suggest include the high cost of maintaining a home, a present home design's incompatibility with present needs, the previous departure from the neighborhood of family and friends, the decline of safety and security in the neighborhood, the prospect's inability to drive and visit physicians, shopping, and other services, and so forth. Marketing representatives should be able to present a brief history of the facility itself, as well as a history and business and financial summary of the developer or management company. AARP suggests that prospective residents ask these probing questions, such as, "To check the financial stability further, ask for a copy of the most recent audited financial statement. Is the operator meeting his debt service and operating costs, with sufficient reserves to offset unanticipated expenses in the future?" Sales representatives should be prepared to answer these questions appropriately.

THE SALES STAFF. The relative newness and the hybrid nature of upscale retirement living offers neither a pool of well-trained sales individuals nor well-known traits and sales behaviors necessary to do the job. Given the paucity of experienced salespeople and knowledge about what it takes to become one, the familiar checklists of high energy, empathy, self-confidence, high ego drive, a love of money, and so on are useless. In fact, many effective sales representatives in retirement settings are quiet, reserved, modest, and unpretentious. Yet it *is* important for a marketing representative to be well-motivated and effectively trained. Selling in this industry emphatically requires that the sales staff build a strong relationship with the prospective residents—the staff needs to understand the wants and needs of older adults.

If the proper care and sales technique is employed, market propensities suggest that older adults will accept smaller living units, pay more than initially intended, and respond positively to lifestyle-oriented sales approaches. They do not respond to a sense of urgency about purchases in general, especially not for such a serious decision. The resultant extended time period needed to close the

sale is usually *not* met with similar competition—almost half of residents who move to retirement settings do so without shopping for other seniors facilities, and the major competition faced by a congregate community is the prospect's own home. A 1990 survey (AARP 1990) showed that 86 percent of older adults are very satisfied with their housing, up from 78 percent in 1986. Moreover, these older people are thinking ahead in terms of staying in their present homes, not in terms of retirement facility housing—the same survey found that 65 percent anticipate needing help in the future with outdoor home maintenance, up from 40 percent in 1986. These older adults do not intend on relying on family for their housing needs; they choose to live alone and prefer it that way.

Most retirement counselors range from 30 to 65 years of age and have previous experience in life insurance sales, social work, health-care administration, and jobs requiring working with other people and good listening skills. Salespeople with good records as closers are best, but the hard-sell approach is known *not* to work. Indeed, it is more important that a prospective employee for retirement residential sales understand the intangibles of selling. Previous real estate sales experience is not necessary when selecting retirement counselors, and some developer/owners prefer to select people who live in and around the community—whatever their background—they may have excellent contacts already, and they give the project local credibility. Former officers in local charity or civic organizations who are looking for new careers are particularly desirable sales agents. Sales staff training must include modules on good listening skills, ability to overcome objections, flawless product knowledge, and excellent knowledge of the municipality surrounding the retirement community.

EVALUATING THE SALES EFFORT. Clearly the bottom-line standard in evaluating the sales effort is measuring the average number of new residents per month. However, several enabling factors—advertising, promotion, and publicity, for instance—will affect this

standard. So how should an evaluation system be designed? First, develop a master lead bank, either manual or electronic, with every lead inputted into the system. Then develop a daily call sheet and require that the sales staff record the number of calls completed, which should be compared against the target objectives. Next, measure the number of calls made against the number of appointments booked and convened, and against preset goals, and measure the number of appointments eventually leading to paid deposits against budgeted projections. Finally, measure the number of deposit payers who convert to close and move in against projections. While this is a suggested system for a new development, modifications can be made to accommodate an existing retirement community as well.

REFERENCES

American Association for Retired Persons. 1990. *Understanding Senior Housing for the 1990s.* Washington, D.C.: American Association for Retired Persons.

Gaynes, N. 1988. Targeting Opportunities in Over-Built Markets. *Retirement Housing Report.* May: 4–7.

Kotler, P. 1988. *Marketing Management: Analysis, Planning and Control.* 5th ed. Englewood Cliffs, N.J.: Prentice-Hall.

Meister, S., and Kitchen, J. 1988. Marketing Lessons from CCRC Residents. *Retirement Housing Report.* Volume 2, Number 12.

Rohrer, R., and Bibb, R. 1986. Marketing the CCRC Challenge. *Contemporary Long-Term Care.* May: 45–48.

SUGGESTED READINGS

American Association of Retired Persons. 1985. *Your Home, Your Choice: A Workbook for Older People and Their Families.* Washington, D.C.: American Association for Retired Persons.

Newland, J. 1990. Promotion: How to Get the Right People to Know Who You Are and What You Can Do. *Spectrum.* October: 22–27.

Wise, L. 1989. Reaching the Children of Seniors—Demographic Realities and Successful Marketing Strategies for Retirement Communities. *Spectrum.* December: 6–9.

CHAPTER FIVE

PLANNING RETIREMENT FACILITIES

WHITE HORSE VILLAGE,
EDGEMONT TOWNSHIP,
PENNSYLVANIA

Hard surfaces, exposed ductwork, and unfinished woods underscore the dining room's cheerful mood. (Architecture: Bower Lewis Thrower/Architects; interiors: Merlino Interior Design; carpet: U.S. Axminster; furniture: D. Becker & Sons, L&B Contract Industries; fabric: Duralee Fabrics Ltd.; millwork: Snavely Co.; lighting: Lightolier; flatware: Oneida Silversmiths; glassware: Libbey; china: Jackson; photo: Richard Quindry.)

The successful outcome of any type of retirement facility development depends in large measure on adequate and thorough planning. Many an ill-fated project had its beginnings in poor planning, with only vague notions of the exact services to be delivered to the future consumers. The necessary planning includes the involvement and expertise of various consultants, whose recommendations will ultimately affect how management and operations are able to service future residents. These consultants' specialties include the following: management services, architectural services, equipment planning, medical services, foodservice, marketing, financial services, construction management, and interior space planning and design.

It is always helpful to the architect and the designer when the owner or developer has definitive information (or at least a good idea) on exactly how the delivery of services will be accomplished on the project. It is also helpful for the owner or developer to define his or her expectations of service levels and of the specific tasks to be delivered within the physical confines of a new facility. This specific information will assist the architectural, design, and engineering teams in producing a physical facility that accommodates all of the required service functions.

Much of this necessary information can be gleaned from good market and demographic studies, as well as from a financial feasibility study in the market area. A feasibility study may only indicate whether there is actually a potential market for the project. It may give a profile of the potential end user of the retirement living product or service. After careful evaluation of the market and demographic analysis and the financial feasibility study, an owner should then formulate a written plan and a services program of exactly what services will actually be offered to future residents. These ideas will give specific direction and vision to the planners, architects, and designers, and will hasten the development of a structural design geared toward the anticipated aesthetic and functional needs of the end users.

Many veteran or first-time owner/ developers make the mistake of not involving an experienced management consultant at the onset of planning for a facility. This is important, because although many owners may bring financial backing or other knowledge to the project, they are often novices in the specifics of service delivery in a retirement project. Indeed, the first few months of poor service delivery on a project due to the physical plant or inadequate staff training can hasten the demise of an otherwise promising project, and it can take years of excellent service delivery to dispel the bad taste left by a few initial months of poor service.

**FREEDOM PLAZA,
SUN CITY, ARIZONA**

Silk plants dress up the setting
of this contemporary dining room.
(Architecture: Freedom Group Inc.;
interiors: Merlino Interior Design
Associates; silk plants: Alves
Flowers; chairs: Hickory Furniture
with fabric by Kravet and
Naugahyde; tables: The Chair
Factory; wallcovering: Maharam;
lighting: Winona; window
treatment: Dazian's Inc.; ceiling:
Armstrong; ceiling fan: Casablanca;
carpet: Durkan Patterned Carpet;
photo: James Cowlin.)

**PARKLANE,
SALT LAKE CITY, UTAH**

Although each of the 94 dwelling
units is equipped with its own
kitchen, the most residents take
their meals in the dining room.
(Architecture: Mole/Huss/Money;
interiors: Life Designs; tables:
Loewenstein; chairs: Schafer with
fabric by Decorloom; planters:
Pyromedia; wallcovering: Keith
McCoy; photo: Michael
Schoenfeld.)

Word-of-mouth referral is one of the strongest motivators for demand-driven purchase decisions in the senior living industries. This example will illustrate the point: When an ethnic couple made the long-awaited decision to purchase and move into a seniors facility, the very next thing they did was convince their friends, especially those who lived in their neighborhood and who went to the same church, to join them in their new residence. It is to an owner's advantage to be allied with a professional who is not only *educated* but *experienced* in seniors management issues. Such a person's wealth of knowledge in congregate living options and medical service delivery is an invaluable resource and will save significant amounts of money in the long run.

THE DESIGN DEVELOPMENT TEAM

A retirement community, in addition to providing residence and life-style support for a seniors population, is a business entity. Many unsuccessful projects are designed and built with no concept of the services that need to be delivered and the support required to deliver them. Often the owner/developer has no notion of work flow, space proximities, or the exact roles and functions of personnel. Designing a facility in an information vacuum is at best a guessing game. A highly skilled team is therefore needed to address issues of space allocation, adjacencies of functions, systems designs, furnishings and equipment planning, and the flexibility to meet future needs.

DEVELOPER. The developer may be the owner, or may be employed by the owner to administer the development of the project. When this sort of arrangement exists, the developer often guides the owner with the help of a financial consultant to determine the financial feasibility of a potential project. The developer may oversee the incorporation of an owner's vision of a project into the facility's actual design and construction, and may also be able to recommend other experienced consultants for the project. A

developer should also be responsible for knowledge of local zoning, codes, and officials.

FINANCIAL CONSULTANT. The financial consultant guides an owner or developer through the actual financing needs of a project. This will be concerned with potential market needs and other demographic issues made apparent by a feasibility study, and will advise on the practicality of a proposed venture weighed against debt service, possible market trends, and fluctuations.

DEMOGRAPHIC CONSULTANT. The demographic consultant is responsible for compilation of demographic data about potential end users in a given market area, often including information on age, sex, marital status, income level, experience and education levels, exposure to proposed product or service, personal preferences, propensities for spending, perceived values and interests, and so forth. This information is valuable in formulating a project program for development of architectural and service programs.

MARKET RESEARCH CONSULTANT. The market research consultant and the demographic consultant may be the same individual. However, some situations may require a more sophisticated analysis, including a stratified random

HEATHERWOOD AT KINGS WAY, YARMOUTH, MASSACHUSETTS

ABOVE: The architects incorporated white clapboard and a widow's walk to capture the original flavor of the old-time whaling community on Cape Cod. (Architecture: Woo & Williams; interiors: Design 1 Interiors; photo: Cymie Payne.)

RIGHT: A woodsy Cape Cod view is the focal point of the dining room. (Architecture: Woo & Williams; interior design: Design 1 Interiors; tables: Shelby Williams; carpet: Milliken; window treatments: Designer Workroom Services with Artmark fabric; Flatware: DJ/Oneida; glassware: Libbey; china: Syracuse; chairs: Shelby Williams with Kravet fabrics on front and back, Clark & Burchfield vinyl on seats; photo: Cymie Payne.)

sample of the proposed market area, to determine the market area's specific needs in both product and services packages. The market research consultant can also predict move-in propensity, which drastically affects profitability and cash flow during the initial rent/lease period.

ARCHITECT. The architect's responsibility is to consult with the owner/developer on proper site planning and utilization, zoning requirements, structural types, and structural feasibility. The architect is also responsible for creating a physical structure to accommodate the functional programming requirements of the owner, and for subcontracting other consultants in the areas of mechanical engineering (heating, ventilating and air conditioning, plumbing, and other systems), structural engineering (calculation of structural loads to determine appropriateness of structural materials and safety requirements with regard to seismic and fire codes and soil conditions, rain, snow load, wind sheer,

heat factors, and so on), and electrical engineering (electricity and lighting requirements, communications and information systems, alarm systems, and so on). The architect is also responsible for generating documents and specifications for use by the contractor and other trades during the construction phase of the project.

EQUIPMENT PLANNER. The role of equipment planner is often handled by several separate consultants, whose expertise may include kitchen planning, laundry planning, medical systems planning, office systems planning, records storage planning, physical therapy equipment planning, maintenance equipment planning, and so forth. In addition to planning, each equipment planner is responsible for the generation and documentation of specifications and budget development of his or her specific area of expertise. If necessary, the equipment planner should be able to offer recommendations to an owner/developer for alternative specifications.

THE RENAISSANCE,
AUSTIN, TEXAS

The private dining room, off the main dining area, provides a place for families to gather. (Architect: Good Fulton & Farrell; interiors: ABV & Associates; main dining room tables, chairs: Stylerite; dining chair fabrics: Robert Allen; chandeliers: Tom Thumb Lighting; wall upholstery: Robert Allen; photo: Peter Paige.) Photography: James Cowlin.

CONSTRUCTION MANAGER. The construction manager, who is hired by and works for the owner/developer, often works in conjunction with a construction cost estimator to bid accurately from construction documents, thereby obtaining an accurate cost estimate of a project's construction costs. This same individual manages and monitors actual project costs against projected costs throughout the project. A construction manager weighs available resources, including labor, within scheduled time constraints to guide progress on a project. He or she should not only be an ombudsman for and with the general contractor, but should be an advocate for the owner/developer.

INTERIOR DESIGNER. The interior designer is a consultant called upon to assist the owner and architect in the development of interior space detailing. The designer also develops final specifications for finish materials on walls, floors, ceilings, window coverings, and cabinetry, and will develop, from the owner's original program, space planning of interior furnishings, including furniture, millwork, artwork, accessories, and plantscaping. Occasionally, a designer will work with subconsultants to develop final published specifications for the aforementioned furnishings. Throughout all of this, the interior designer's goal is to ensure that functional criteria are met in fulfilling the needs of the program for the project. The designer will often work in tandem with the equipment planner to provide the owner with a comprehensive plan for a facility's moveable contents, or *FF&E* items (furnishings, fixtures and equipment). The interior designer is also responsible for the furnishings' and finishes' adherence to local codes for fire, health, and safety.

FOOD MANAGEMENT CONSULTANT. The food management consultant, or food facilities design consultant, can be an independent consultant or a representative of the foodservice management contract company who will operate the leased food services for the owner. The food management consultant offers expertise and recommendations on work flow for foodservice tasks and personnel requirements, and identifies key challenges and solutions for the receiving, storing, transferring, processing, delivering and serving of food. Waste handling and removal are under this person's purview as well. A qualified food management consultant will make recommendations to an owner for the most efficient and flexible kitchen equipment components that can service a variety of menu needs with thought for future trends in food and beverage service. The food management consultant should also be qualified to specify and publish for the owner a comprehensive listing of competitive pricing on foodservice equipment. Specifications should include all necessary information to procure and install the various components, including electrical load requirements, plumbing and venting requirements, fire extinguishing requirements, local waste disposal requirements, and critical path requirements on phased delivery and installation relative to construction phasing.

DIRECTOR OF NURSING (DON). In the case of a long-term care facility, especially a skilled nursing facility or specialty units for long term care, an experienced nursing director is an important asset in early planning. The nursing director is normally the spokesperson for the medical staff of a facility, although, on occasion, a medical director

MEADOWOOD RETIREMENT
COMMUNITY, VALLEY
FORGE, PENNSYLVANIA

At the nursing station in the skilled care facility, the colors and millwork design lend a touch of homeyness and warmth. (Architecture: CS&D Architects; interiors: Life Designs; bench seating: Link Taylor; task seating: Artoplex; carpet: Burtco; planters: Granite Mill; console tables: Lane; weathervane: Good Directions; lamp: Joseph's Own; photo: Michael Schoenfeld.)

supervises health-care delivery. It is the DON who will ultimately manage the health-care delivery and business aspects of the facility on a day-to-day basis. The DON can give valuable information on specific patient requirements, health-care staff task requirements, and real-life insight into actual practices of health-care residents and staff, all of which is helpful to an owner in determining the best delivery of health-care service and value to residents. A nursing director can also determine practical advantages and disadvantages, propose design solutions for functional and physiological needs, and consult with physicians and other providers of medical services providers to determine preferred or more efficient methods of health-care delivery.

FACILITY MANAGEMENT CONSUL-TANT. The facility management consultant is often employed by the owner to administer the operational and business administration needs of the facility. This is particularly true of one-time or first-time developers, who may not have expertise in delivery of services in the seniors market. The facility management consultant, who should have considerable managerial experience in successful seniors facilities, can give recommendations on personnel requirements, phased hiring needs, office setup, security

THE HEARTWOOD, TACOMA, WASHINGTON

In the administrator's office, blue is used for a soothing effect, so that residents will not be intimidated. (Architecture: Merritt & Pardini; interiors: Hendrix Interiors; carpet: Mohawk; wallcovering: Wallprice; window treatments: Verosol Pleated Shades; tables and chairs: Hammer of California; fabrics: Robert Allen Fabrics; photo: Mark Ricketts Photography.)

arrangements, revenue and overhead projections, resident assistance, and so forth. Often, the facility management consultant is retained by the owner/developer and may become the facility manager or administrator at a later date.

SALES OR MARKETING CONSULTANT. The presale phase of a project generally is the most important phase in determining a project's future viability. For this reason, a sales or marketing consultant, or even an independent marketing group, is invaluable. The marketing consultant can help an owner/developer with recommendations on how to package services and physical products desirably for buyers in a local market. This pertains not only to presale, but to ongoing sales, leases, or rentals. It is vital to involve marketing personnel throughout the planning and design phases for two reasons: to ensure that the design theme and direction are compatible with the expectations of the market, and to educate marketers on the realities of what can actually be offered to end users from a financial-feasibility perspective. This ensures that expectations do not diverge from market realities.

WORKING METHODOLOGY AND PROJECT PROTOCOL

An important factor throughout the planning and design phases is working methodology and protocol between owner and consultants, as well as between the various consultants themselves. These relationships generally will be dictated by the contractual arrangements established by the owner.

In a typical scenario, the owner contracts total responsibility for project development to the developer, who in turn either contracts directly with all consultants individually or arranges for direct contractual responsibility to the owner, who is often the funding source. Occasionally, a master contract may be set up, under which all consultants are subcontracted to either the architect or the developer for the development of a complete package, to be delivered to the owner upon completion of the project.

Because the successful outcome of a retirement project is dependent on the maintenance of good working relationships among the several consultants, it is imperative that work scopes and project responsibilities are clearly defined at the onset of the project, that all principals and consultants understand the portions of the project for which they will be responsible, and that all parties understand accountability, reporting protocol, and scheduling.

It is important that decision makers are identified to all consultant groups. It is also imperative that those to whom the quality of the completed product is important arrange for regular interaction between themselves and the team of consultants for review, comment, and approvals. Since most consultants have the desire to perform well, it is important that each discipline represented on a project be regarded as a valuable entity in the success of the completed project. This is accomplished by consistent and regular communication, clear definition of expectations, flexible problem solving, and the owner or developer taking the time for thoughtful review and the responsibility for the final sign-off.

Since many projects are conceived and designed well in advance of the start of physical construction, it may surprise first-time developers or owners to realize that planning decisions made during the conceptual phases (or at other given times during development) may not become physical realities for four to eight years. Conceptual planning decisions are made for a population of residents and staff who are nameless but who nonetheless need thoughtful planning for their future residences and work spaces. Indeed, the more ambiguity that can be avoided in programming, planning, and design specifics, the better the probability of a favorable outcome.

ARCHITECTURAL PLANNING CONSIDERATIONS

Architectural planning considerations for retirement facilities will vary according to the market area and market segment for which the project is intended, the

planning and programming, the availability of financing, and the physical characteristics of the specific location. Key issues in the planning of a campus and a residential facility with required specialty units include the following:

SITE SELECTION. The selection of a site for the location of a seniors facility presents special challenges. Many factors should be weighed, including location of the site relative to primary market prospects, topography, availability of utilities, zoning and neighborhood requirements, availability of transportation, security, availability of consumer conveniences, solar orientation, land availability, and land cost.

In addition, many questions concerning access issues and market preferences need to be answered: How far will residents need to relocate to move into the facility? Should the facility be near an urban center, or in a more suburban, residential location? Will it be near major transportation arteries? Will it be near medical, dental, and social services? Will it be near consumer services, such as stores, dry cleaners, libraries, gas stations, and so on? Will it be near community and religious places and services? If not, will transportation be available and convenient to residents? Will the site be compatible with local neighborhood needs? Will occupants feel comfortable in the new neighborhood? Will landmarks make the facility easy to locate from a major highway? Will there be traffic hazards to negotiate? Will the entrance to the project be easily found? Will the approach to the buildings be logical and easily traveled?

TOPOGRAPHY. Topography generally dictates the type of structure and master plan or layout. The type of structure and the amount of site preparation affect the construction cost. These issues relate to the physical structure itself, while structure layout, dictates how an individual resident will get around *within* the facility or on its campus.

A steeply sloped site will often dictate a multi-tiered, vertical layout, usually necessitating stairs, ramps, or elevators to traverse the steep grades.

BRANDON WOODS OF MANLIUS

ELDER CARE SERVICES INCORPORATED
MANLIUS, NEW YORK MARCH 1988

ENGELBRECHT AND GRIFFIN ARCHITECTS P.C.
C. WILLIAM DUHN ENVIRONMENTAL ENGINEERING
THEODORE BRICKMAN CO. LANDSCAPE ARCHITECTS

MASTER PLAN

SCALE IN FEET
0   100   200   400

MARCH 9, 1988

SITE SECTION

SITE PLAN

NORTH

Moreover, vertical construction is more costly than flatter layouts. While many gently sloped campuses are functional and most effective—indeed, many wooded or mountainous sloped sites can have amenities of outdoor beauty that cannot be replicated—more steeply graded sites are not preferable. A steep grade warrants careful study.

On a flat site, almost any type of structure can be built. The most common is a one- or two-story structure spread out over many acres. Although a campus of this type has a minimal amount of ramps, stairs, and elevators to negotiate, residents often must traverse lengthy distances, and a less optimum building circulation pattern is sometimes dictated as well. One advantage of a flatter site is that large outdoor activity areas can be created.

ZONING AND NEIGHBORHOODS.
There are many challenges presented when an owner/developer begins plans to integrate a multiple-unit retirement development into an existing neighborhood. Local city and county jurisdictions have requirements that will affect the efficient design of a site and its use. While it is advantageous to locate a facility in a desirable residential neighborhood, a developer must also consider the demands that the facility will place upon the neighborhood in such areas as parking, traffic volume, fire protection, and demands on water, sewer, natural gas, and electrical power resources.

Population-density factors will be the prime consideration for planning boards for sites proposed in residential neighborhoods, because higher-density housing places higher demands on such

BRANDON WOODS
AT MANLIUS,
MANLIUS, NEW YORK

The dramatic, circular thoroughfare accommodates the area's natural slope (see cross section, bottom), with the congregate community located at the top of the hill and development's other structures distributed in clusters around the site. (Courtesy of Elder Care Services, Inc.)

FAIRWAYS AT BROOKLINE VILLAGE, STATE COLLEGE, PENNSYLVANIA

The facility is nestled on a hilly ridge next to Nittany Mountain, which forced architect Robert L. Beers to cut into an embankment to provide level terrain on which to build. Entrances to all buildings are on ground level for wheelchair access. In this corridor lounge, and throughout The Fairways, the carpeting is a tightly woven low pile that ensures smooth going for wheelchairs, canes, and feet alike. (Architecture: Robert L. Beers, AIA, Architects; interiors: Merlino Interior Design Associates; carpet: Bigelow; wallcovering: Vicrtex, Sanitas Wallcovering; fabrics: Coral of Chicago; furniture: O-Asian; photo: Richard Quindry.)

community services as hospitals. A seniors facility however, is often granted special consideration, because it does not place heavy demands on road systems, traffic (except during construction) or currently existing school systems, yet increases the tax base significantly. With this in mind, many jurisdictions will review how a planned development will fit into their long-range, community master plans for residential, commercial, industrial, and mixed-use areas. A developer often will be required to commit millions of dollars in general improvements to services (and perhaps utilities) and approachways of a project before approval is granted.

TRANSPORTATION. Because of the impaired vision and health of many elderly persons, it is not feasible to assume that

all residents will be able to provide their own transportation to such basic services as medical facilities and other clinics, churches, temples, synagogues, and shopping centers. These services are often provided on campus, but residents will still need to travel off the campus for various reasons, such as visiting friends or family, attending community events, attending university classes, and the like. The availability of public and supplemental private transportation is important—access to community bus lines, subways, and railway systems should be considered. Some facilities also offer private shuttle-bus or limousine service for residents on a scheduled or privately requested basis, which presents an overhead factor to consider while planning site-location and operational budgets—in short, is this service

something that the market will sufficiently appreciate and pay for?

SECURITY. Of prime importance to most older adults is their physical security. Many seniors feel at particular risk to being accosted, mugged, or otherwise attacked. While selecting a site, an owner/developer should consider what security provisions will accommodate the expectations of the prospective resident market. Obviously, high-crime neighborhoods should be avoided when choosing a building site. If a suitable site cannot be located in a safe neighborhood, structural provisions must be made so that indoor and outdoor activities can be maintained by campus residents without fear of physical harm. Locating a retirement facility in a high-crime area will also require added security staffing, and the exterior design should give residents a sense of security and comfort, especially at ground level.

Regardless of neighborhood type, landscaping and structural design must avoid the creation of dark areas and blind spots. Windows and doors must provide air circulation and be secure from outside intrusion. A system of interior checkpoints should be established to screen entrants to the building, and routine security inspections should be conducted by personnel on foot or by video surveillance. Residents may appreciate a routine knock on their doors, or a phone call, at least once daily, contributing to a feeling of extended family throughout the facility.

INTERIOR PLANNING CONSIDERATIONS

PROGRAMMING TO THE NEEDS OF THE MARKET. When planning a facility's services and physical layout, the design team (the owner/developer, a management representative, the architect, an interior designer, and other consultants as previously mentioned) must

THE ROSSMOOR REGENCY, LAGUNA BEACH, CALIFORNIA

A large porte cochere shelters the lobby entrance and enhances the sense of arrival. The property's symbol, a sculptural steel globe, is meant to reflect the sophisticated tastes of its globetrotting residents—the facility aims to attract an affluent, active bunch of seniors. Its inducements range from the Rolls Royce always parked outside to the attractive site, close to prime shopping and recreational areas. (Architecture: Terry Architects; interiors: Jung Designs; photo: Milroy/McAleer)

keep the needs of the target market in focus. For instance, the needs of a congregate housing resident in his early 50s will be far different from those of a skilled nursing resident in her middle 80s. Likewise, an assisted living resident's needs will be different than those of a resident with Alzheimer's Disease.

A retirement facility must support its residents in both their physical condition and their life-style. Within the segments of resident types, there will also be need for variety as well as for flexible options available to residents. For example, one 65-year-old resident may require shallow, upright seating, while another resident of the same age may prefer a softer, deeper piece of furniture. One resident may require consistent placement of handrails throughout the facility, while another may be 20 years from needing the same feature. Accommodations within a facility to meet a wide range of physical needs must be considered and put into the program at the beginning of the project. Aesthetic requirements and local taste preferences must also be considered at this point. All of these considerations make it very important that the design team members have good working relationships with one another, keep focused on the same goals and criteria, and plan for the needs of several generations of residents of varying health.

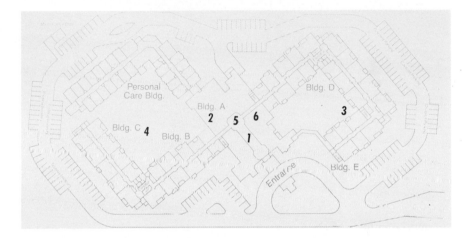

THE RENAISSANCE, SHERMAN, TEXAS

As this site plan shows, The Renaissance is laid out around two courtyards for security and a sense of privacy. In the main building, a glass-walled elevator allows residents to look out over the two-and-a-half story lobby colonnade. Buildings B, C, D, and E house residential units for fully independent living. Legend: 1. Lobby colonnade. 2. Commons building housing dining and other community facilities. 3. West courtyard. 4. East courtyard. 5. Elevator. 6. Activity rooms. (Architecture: Archon.)

THE HEARTWOOD, TACOMA, WASHINGTON

Since 70 percent of the facility's residents are in wheelchairs, the tables in the dining room are arranged with ample space in between. (Architecture: Merritt & Pardini; interiors: Hendrix Interiors; carpet: Charleston Carpets; wood floor: Permagrain Products; chandeliers: Seattle Lighting; chairs: Hammer of California with fabric by Robert Allen Fabrics; vinyl by Wolf Gordon; tables and bases: Spectrum Furniture Company; photo: Mark Ricketts Photography.)

In the dining room, which seats
200, sturdy armchairs with firm
seats ensure the comfort of all
diners. (Architecture: Terry
Architects; interiors: Jung Designs;
draperies: Fabric Treasures;
dining chairs: Flexsteel; carpet:
Carpets from London; dining
tables: West Coast Industries;
chandeliers: Feldman Lighting;
consoles, end tables: Lane; photo:
Milroy/McAleer.)

BUILDING LAYOUT. Regardless of structure type or plan direction (horizontal or vertical), building layouts can usually be produced to support the program needs of the residents. Indoor and outdoor spaces should be established with a hierarchical methodology, with private, semiprivate, and public spaces organized in a rational fashion throughout the campus.

Developing a space hierarchy does *not* imply that all spaces need be boxes. Similarly, such a scheme does not preclude the use of creative solutions for the functional separation or integration of space. How a building is situated on a site can affect the efficiency of these design solutions, as can topography, solar orientation, local set-back requirements, and so forth. Taking these factors into account, all resident spaces, whether indoor or outdoor, should provide opportunities for socialization and positive participation, or for seclusion or rest. All spaces, regardless of type, should be laid out to achieve a sense of familiarity, rather than confusion. The goal should be to create a sense of community, with subcommunities existing within the whole.

Outdoor spaces can create opportunities for residents to stay in contact with natural light, seasonal changes, and fresh air. They also create informal opportunities for observing others, often giving individuals a way to participate vicariously, especially if they are physically or socially impaired or intimidated.

Provisions for seating, shading, wind barriers, landscaping, and acoustic barriers should all be considered where appropriate.

Landscaping that provides high contrast in form and color value is important. Landscaped areas should not include elements so high that they create security, orientation, or surveillance problems. Waist height is ideal for shrubbery, and treetop massing should begin at above 6 feet (1.8 meters). Careful orientation of building forms and landscaping can actually create pockets where seasons can be extended, allowing people to enjoy sitting or walking in comfort, shielded from wind, sun, and other elements. These same environments can also be created within indoor atria.

PARKLANE, SALT LAKE CITY, UTAH

LEFT: Everything flows off the Parklane's central atrium: Plants abound, while umbrellas, street lamps, and benches add to the parklike atmosphere, creating cozy conversation points to avoid the overly spacious feeling of the atrium. (Architecture: Mole/Huss/Money; interiors: Life Designs; umbrellas: Terra; chairs: L&B Contract Industries; benches: Melnor; planters: International Terra Cotta; laminate tables: C&H; flooring tile: American Olean; photo: Michael Schoenfeld.)

TOP RIGHT: In the corridors, the handrail on the right side was designed to correspond to the chair rail on the opposite side. Sconces provide soft, indirect lighting. The atrium is intentionally left in darkness to create an outdoor effect in the evening. Unfortunately, set-back requirements for the facility's urban setting left no room for outdoor landscaping. (Architecture: Mole/Huss/Money; interiors: Life Designs; carpet: Whitehall; wallcovering: Winfield Designs; lighting: Vista; signage: Stippich/Giraffics; paint: Sherwin Williams; photo: Michael Schoenfeld.)

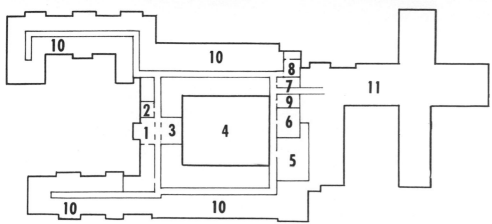

FORWOOD MANOR,
WILMINGTON, DELAWARE

Legend of floor plan: 1. Lobby.
2. Library. 3. Living room.
4. Courtyard. 5. Dining room.
6. Bar/lounge. 7. General store.
8. Game room. 9. Exercise
room. 10. Residential wings.
11. Assisted living and skilled
nursing wing. (Architecture:
Moeckel Carbonell Associates.)

PARKLANE,
SALT LAKE CITY, UTAH

An overhead shot of the atrium offers a glimpse of what residents see from their balconies. For a change of scenery during the day, a buffet lunch is served here. (Architecture: Mole/Huss/Money; interiors: Life Designs; umbrellas: Terra; chairs: L&B Contract Industries; benches: Melnor; planters: International Terra Cotta; laminate tables: C&H; flooring tile: American Olean; photo: Michael Schoenfeld.)

Major walkways should be 6 feet (1.8 meters) wide; minor walkways should be half this width. The basic rule of thumb for walkways is to create enough space for two wheelchair-bound individuals to pass one another while going in opposite directions.

Consideration of sidewalk and stair texture is important, as is avoiding locating walkways in areas that will receive heavy drifting snow, rain, or sand. Walkway intersections should be wider than normal walkways, to allow for socializing and wheelchair maneuvering. Corners should be gently curved. Pathways should provide for shortcuts, since people tend to take them anyway, thereby destroying the planned landscaped appearance.

For stairs and level changes, at least three risers should be used, but no more than 10 per flight. Risers should be of uniform height, and stairs and ramps should have increased illumination. Handrails should be provided on both sides, as well as down the center if the stairway is very wide.

When designing specific types of interior spaces within a structure, acuity-limitation principles dictate design solutions. General rules of thumb cannot always be applied, since requirements for, say, a dining room will vary depending on whether the facility is an Alzheimer's unit, a skilled nursing facility,

or whatever. In each case, the users' abilities and limitations will dictate heights, widths, depths, and so forth.

COMMUNITY COHESION. The sense of community that individuals feel in a retirement facility can be dramatically affected by the building's layout and its conduciveness to cohesion. The fear and uncertainty associated with leaving a familiar place and personal belongings and surroundings is probably the single greatest challenge facing marketing and sales personnel when trying to convince prospective residents that they will feel at home in this new location. Many prospective residents also fear becoming a nameless face among hundreds on a new campus. Because of design efficiencies, building structures often do little to assist individuals in feeling any sense of intimacy or individuality in the surroundings, particularly in apartment wings, where many corridors are long tunnels lined by hundreds of repetitive doors with no visual relief or interesting design details. Residents often have no sense of neighborhood—there is no clustering or "podding" of units to form small subcommunities within the whole campus community.

Today, more architects are beginning to understand the need for being acquainted with a handful of neighbors who become friends. Building layout and

design can facilitate this goal—indeed, an entire building's footprint is dictated by the arrangement of living units in relationship to public spaces and walkways. Whether they are congregate living units or independent dwellings, neighborhoods of four to eight dwellings or units can be arranged to face out onto semiprivate common areas that invite mingling, a sense of identity, and caring among a group of neighbors.

Resident entryways within a community can also be excellent places for residents' expressions of individuality. This can be in the form of signage, plantings, furniture, arts and crafts, and so forth. Individuality also provides quick and easy identification and orientation for residents in their wayfinding. Historically, a great deal of facility space was dedicated to corridor sublobbies, to be used by residents as an extension of their private spaces. These spaces were often poorly lit and unfurnished. Also, because they were located in public accessways, they were not conducive to intimate and informal gathering, and consequently were often wasted. Today's facilities provide smaller, out-of-the-way spaces, with a solarium, detailing, and furnishings, and these spaces are used as intended. The solariums give periodic punctuation to corridors and lend a generous amount of natural light, thereby aiding in orientation and wayfinding.

THE SEASONS KENWOOD, CINCINNATI, OHIO

Daylight floods the five-story atrium, where a gently sloping grand staircase encourages residents to climb and remain physically active. Discreetly recessed low-voltage lights illuminate the stairs, while arabesques in the stair carpet design serve as visual cues to the height of the risers. (Architecture: PDT + Co.; interiors: Lynn Wilson Associates, Inc.; carpet: Durkan Patterned Carpet; photo: Eric Hecktor.)

NEWPORT BAY
CONDOMINIUMS,
INDIANAPOLIS, INDIANA

The entrance to each living unit
is detailed with colonial-style
modeling, broken pediments, and
carriage lamps for the effect of
a streetscape. (Architecture:
Wolner Associates; interiors:
Eden Design Associates; carpet:
Bentley; ceramic wall tiles: Gail
Architectural Ceramics; paint:
Benjamin Moore; floor tiles:
Fiandre; photo: Dan Francis,
Marden Photography.)

THE RENAISSANCE,
SHERMAN, TEXAS

This floor plan of a typical
500-square-foot minisuite shows
the generous kitchen, bath,
and storage spaces available at
this facility. Legend: 1. Entry.
2. Kitchen. 3. Bath. 4. Closet.
5. Linen storage. 6. Sleeping
room. 7. Living room.
(Architecture: Archon.)

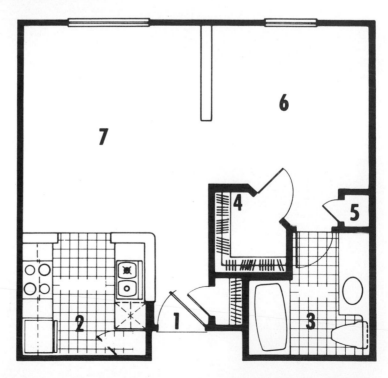

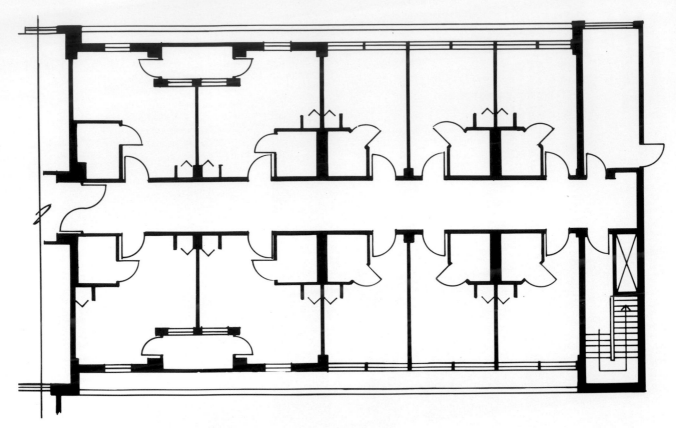

TYPICALLY EFFICIENT
APARTMENT LAYOUT

ABOVE: The emphasis here is on square-footage efficiency—to a fault. Most walls are drawn at right angles, with no space "wasted" on attractive design details. Corridors are straight and similarly monotonous, again with no design relief. This layout, while cost-effective, is uncreative and does nothing to enhance the residents' quality of life. Often referred to as the "rabbit hutch" approach, this style was more common in the 1970s. (Illustration: Douglas Smith/Life Designs.)

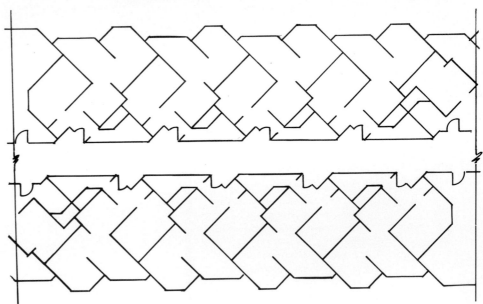

CREATIVE LAYOUT VARIATION

This type of approach, representing a more creative use of square footage, is becoming more common. While many spaces are rotated to take advantage of outside views, consistent use of right angles in most spaces still allows for construction economy. Corridors are given relief with space undulation and design detailing. (Illustration: Douglas Smith/Life Designs.)

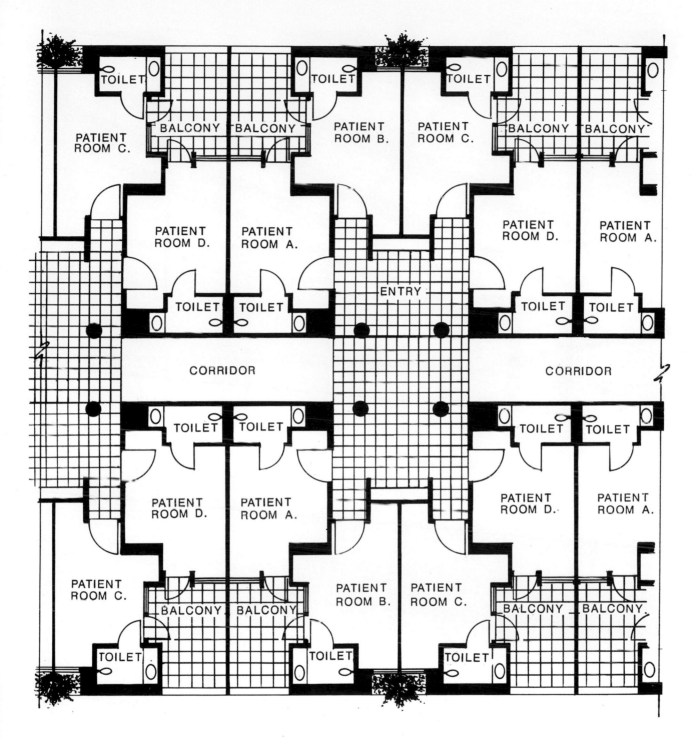

CLUSTER FLOOR PLAN

This layout, in which residents are grouped into pods or clusters, is both creative and efficient. The pods result in subcommunities within the larger facility, helping residents feel a greater sense of personalization in their own "neighborhoods." Every four resident rooms have their own recessed entry, with every two rooms adjoining a balcony. (Illustration: Douglas Smith/Life Designs.)

BEAUMONT, BRYN MAWR, PENNSYLVANIA

LEFT: The cheerful solarium dining area was built out from an exterior wall of the former Austin mansion. It overlooks one of the three-story apartment units adjacent to the main house. Quarry tile, rattan, and chintzlike fabric carry through the breezy outdoor feeling of this space, one of Beaumont's eight distinctive dining environments. Being able to choose a different dining room every night of the week helps alleviate boredom for Beaumont residents. (Architecture: Ann C. Capron; interiors: Arthur Shuster, Inc.; chairs: Shelby William with ACT vinyl seats, back with JD Fabrics; tables: Falcon; flatware: Oneida; glassware: Arcoroc; china: Shenango China; photo: Tom Crane.)

RIGHT: Details of the house's original architecture, such as the wrought iron door grills, molded ceiling beams, and random gray stone walls with limestone trim, add character to the dining porch. (Architecture: Ann C. Capron; interiors: Arthur Shuster, Inc.; chairs: Shelby Williams with ACT vinyl seats, Kravet fabric backs; tables: Falcon; photo: Tom Crane.)

BELOW: Many of Beaumont's commons spaces, including the dining rooms, are housed in the first floor of the original mansion house. Legend: 1. Foyer. 2. Entry lounge. 3. Cocktail lounge. 4. Dining areas. 5. Solarium dining. 6. Women's club room. 7. Employee dining. 8. Kitchen. 9. Music room. (Architecture: Ann C. Capron.)

Programs organized by operational staff can also assist residents in attaining a sense of neighborhood. These programs can encourage pride in group efforts and group identity. For example, small on-site shops—often run by residents—can increase opportunities for socializing and create a sense of being needed and of caring for others. These services may include food and convenience shops, beauty and barber shops, floral and gift shops, packaging and mailing services, craft shops, and so forth. All of these programs may assist residents in feeling like this new place of residence really is their home.

ADJACENCY PLANNING. After the owner/developer, marketing research consultants, and management consultants have settled on a services package (the specific resident activities that need to be planned by the designers) and determined whether it will be offered as a complete bundled package or as a series of à la carte options, the design team begins *adjacency planning*. Simply put, an adjacency plan identifies all activities according to their overlapping similarities and differences.

For example, a chapel, a library, and a day room for sleeping may all require privacy and quiet, but they are quite different in terms of purpose and intended use. Therefore, they could not all utilize the same space. However, a small auditorium might also serve as a chapel; a library might also accommodate a computer area, and so forth. When forming an adjacency plan, the team should always use great foresight in assessing the future needs of the facility and its residents. Moreover, the planners and designers need to plan accordingly for phases of expansion (or reduction) in given areas of use as needs change.

The first stage of an adjacency plan is to identify the activity requirements within a building and assess their special aspects or requirements. For example, several activities may require large amounts of covered, open space, allowing for the free movement of individuals; several other activities may require an area with work tops, a sink, and surroundings that cannot be harmed by messy activities; still others may require a covered area with flexible seating, a stage, and a lectern, while another may require privacy and quiet.

The second stage of an adjacency plan is to locate tasks in physical relationship to one another by the use of circles, called a *bubble diagram*. The sizes of the circles in a bubble diagram vary depending on the number of individuals that must be accommodated for the activity's needs. For example, a space serving the limited interests of a few individuals, such as a sewing room, would be represented by a circle or bubble perhaps an inch (2.5 cm) in diameter, while the requirements for a space seating an entire community of 350 persons would be represented by a circle five times wider. Activity bubbles may be subdivided by other activity bubbles, representing overlapping and compatible needs for each area. For example, a 350-person meeting room may also be designed to accommodate dancing, aerobics, staff training, and other larger group activities.

The third stage of adjacency planning is to begin to form more rigid forms by clustering and determining the exact floor areas each activity will require, based on capacity and space requirements for each activity. A pattern of rooms or spaces begins to develop into a preliminary layout plan. At this point, shared requirements, such as the need for plumbing, venting, natural light, acoustics, and so forth, begin to become apparent, and the team will likely find that the coupling of interior space requirements with designated space titles, locations, and services becomes both fascinating and maddening. To the novice planner, it will seem like a giant chess game, fraught with contradictions and complications; to the skilled planner, the handsome benefits and rewards of designing the space also become apparent at this stage.

MEADOWOOD RETIREMENT COMMUNITY, VALLEY FORGE, PENNSYLVANIA

The auditorium space serves as a multifunctional area, accommodating 350 movable and stackable seats and a variety of other activities. A low stage platform is useful for lecture and performing arts activities. (Architecture: CS&D Architects; interiors: Life Designs; photo: Michael Schoenfeld.)

HEATHERWOOD AT KINGS WAY, YARMOUTH, MASSACHUSETTS

ABOVE: Dark mahogany millwork and deep colors make the library a formal yet serene enclave. (Architecture: Woo & Williams; interiors: Design 1 Interiors; chairs: Jenson Custom Furniture; wingback chairs: Italmond; table: Harden; chairside box: Hooker Furniture; lamps: Remington Lamps; carpet: Milliken; art, accessories: Design 1 Interiors; photo: Cymie Payne.)

RIGHT: A fireplace, glowing coral tones, and warm natural light lend the parlor a cozy, convivial ambience. (Architecture: Woo & Williams; interiors: Design 1 Interiors; sofa: Unique Design; chairs, butler table, sofa table: Drexel Heritage; floor lamp: Remington Lamps; area rug: Masland; window treatments: Designer Workroom Services with Pindler & Pindler and Robert Allen fabrics; wallcovering: Kinney Wallcoverings; photo: Cymie Payne.)

BUBBLE DIAGRAM

It is useful to identify intended spaces and their respective functions at the outset of space programming. Approximate square footage data and critical area interrelationships should be noted. (Illustration: Douglas Smith/Life Designs.)

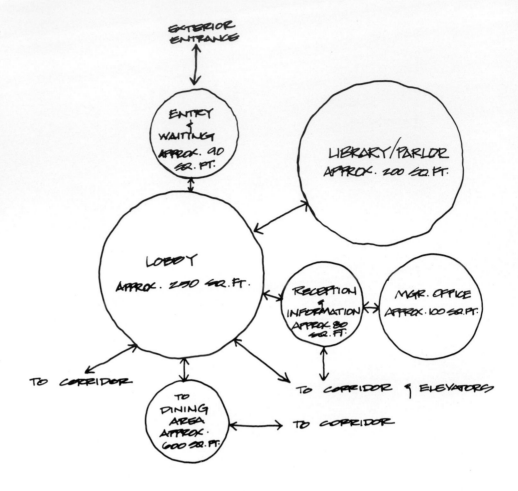

SCHEMATIC FLOOR PLAN

Schematic planning, showing scaled out square footage requirements and spaces located by dependency of functional relationship, represents a progression from the bubble diagram stage. (Illustration: Douglas Smith/Life Designs.)

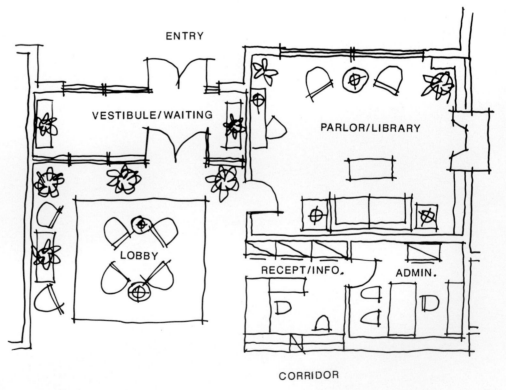

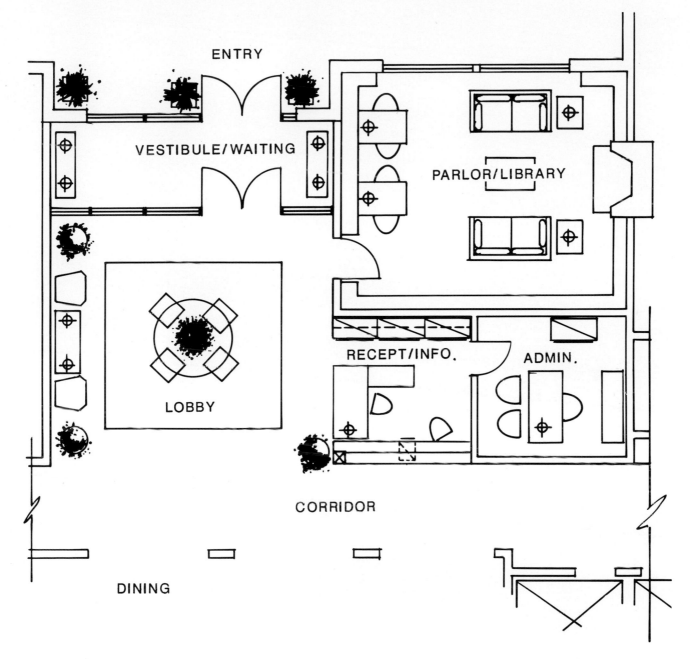

ENTRY

VESTIBULE/WAITING

PARLOR/LIBRARY

LOBBY

RECEPT/INFO.

ADMIN.

CORRIDOR

DINING

The final stage of an adjacency plan is to finalize room locations and sizes. The architect can then draft a floor plan, complete with doors, windows, HVAC plans, ceiling heights, floor level changes, plumbing, lighting, and electrical requirements, and so forth. With room sizes and shapes then determined, the equipment planner and interior designer can begin to plan for equipment and furnishings requirements and further refine the interior details of each space, and the mechanical engineers can begin to plan how utilities services will be programmed and designed for each room.

THEME. Theme is the term used to describe the aesthetic styling of a facility. In everyday use, most of us are familiar with such terms as *country, southwestern, tropical, colonial, French, English*, and so on. These, of course, are idiomatic derivatives or jargon used to describe a look, feeling, period, or style. Theme, on the other hand, denotes the styling *essence* of a facility. The goal here is for the exterior or architectural styling to be compatible with and complementary to the interior styling, and vice versa. The presence or absence of a logical and consistent theme throughout a facility

FINAL FLOOR PLAN

This stage, in which the layout is shown in the form of hardline documents ready for construction, completes the process of conceptual planning. (Illustration: Douglas Smith/Life Designs.)

is often the best indicator of whether a design team maintained a common purpose with clearly stated goals and good communications throughout the planning and development phases of the project. In the worst cases, some retirement facilities lead one to wonder if the owner/developer, architect, designer, or contractor ever spoke with one another throughout the project. Other facilities invite conjecture as to what period of history, or style, was being considered as one passes over the threshold of each doorway—while an eclectic mixture of styles may be valid in some cases, a different theme in each room usually gives mixed signals to a prospective market segment.

Theme selection is usually based on the preferences and anticipated acceptance level of prospective residents of the targeted market. Fine-tuning the subtleties and nuances of a theme to meet expectations of local residents, called *regionalizing*, presents a common ground with which local residents can relate and feel comfortable. This is not to say that a

stylized or updated version of a theme cannot add new twists to a traditionally accepted theme for a given area—depending on the rigidity or openness of a given market, many new ideas can be promoted. In some markets, a conservative clientele may appreciate innovations in functional aspects of a design, as long as they are cloaked in a traditional detail or finish.

When selecting a theme for a facility, *general* acceptance level is the key criterion. While many of us may be familiar with some retired individuals who lived for decades in a heavily traditional and conservative area of the country and then sold all their belongings and relocated to a tropical or desert area and started a new life, these are exceptions and do not reflect the norm. Design, therefore, should be focused for the rule, not for the exception.

Studies show that because retired individuals generally wish to remain near extended family and friends, residents within urban and suburban areas are usually drawn from a radius of 8 to 30

FAIRWAYS AT BROOKLINE VILLAGE, STATE COLLEGE, PENNSYLVANIA

Floral carpeting and cozily arranged nineteenth-century-style furniture help to deinstitutionalize the main lobby. (Architecture: Robert L. Beers, AIA, Architects; interiors: Merlino Interior Design Associates; carpet: Charleston Carpets; wallcovering: Genon Vinyl Wallcovering; fabrics: Pindler & Pindler; lighting: Lightolier; artwork: Franklin Picture Co.; furniture: Madison Square, Barrit, Stanton Cooper; photo: Richard Quindry.)

miles (12.9 to 48.3 kilometers); in rural areas, this rule of thumb may be extended to as far as 50 miles (80.5 kilometers). The theme bias should therefore be toward local tastes, with an eye for endurance and immunity to passing trends—keep in mind the sorry number of restaurants and hotels whose themes were the rage three decades ago but now seem comical, unbelievable, or garish.

After (or sometimes in conjunction with) the forming of a project floor plan comes the programming of the functional requirements for each space. The term *functional* denotes any criteria germane to the function, enjoyment, or usage of the space. We will discuss two basic areas

pertaining to this criteria: functional and aesthetic requirements.

FUNCTIONAL REQUIREMENTS. When programming the functional requirements for each space, the team identifies each space's intended activity, along with required equipment or furnishings and any other important factors contributing to the successful accomplishment of those activities. The functional programming requirements of a space can and should be explicit and finite, although they may cover a broad range of issues, such as how high a countertop should be, how firmly a chair will seat an individual, how impact-resistant certain wall

surfaces should be, how handicapped-usable certain hardware shall be, and so on. The facility's future functionality and flexibility will depend on the up-front time spent by the team in determining the functional requirements of each space. The functional program for a pottery crafts room might appear as shown on page 129.

Each room is identified in this manner. This program is then referred to as the standard for that room by all parties on the project. Specific requirements for furnishings, fixtures, finishes, and equipment can then be formulated based on this "shopping list" for the space.

CARLETON-WILLARD VILLAGE, BEDFORD, MASSACHUSETTS

The arts and crafts room is outfitted with sturdy chairs that are comfortable enough to sit in for a long time. On the floor, bold checks of mauve and off-white vinyl tile add spunk to an area reserved for creative activities. (Architect: TRO/The Ritchie Organization; interiors: Adner/Woodman Design; flooring: Armstrong; draperies: Kravet; chairs: Thonet; photo: Robert Mikrut.)

Logan greens and deep burgundies give the cocktail lounge a clublike and hospitable ambience. (Architecture: Bower Lewis Thrower/Architects; interiors: Merlino Interior Design; carpet: Floor Graphix; furniture: L&B Contract Industries, Ello MFG. Co.; D. Becker & Sons; fabric: AAT; millwork: Snavely Co.; signage: Adelphia Graphic Systems; photo: Richard Quindry.)

FUNCTIONAL PROGRAM

Functional planning should leave nothing to chance—try to anticipate every need, especially those that relate specifically to the unique problems faced by seniors.

FUNCTIONAL PROGRAM FOR A POTTERY/CRAFTS ROOM

AREA: Pottery/Crafts Room

ROOM NUMBER: 305

INTENDED CAPACITY:
12 – 14 people

EQUIPMENT REQUIREMENTS:

14 tabletop pottery wheels
 2 full-size throwing wheels (one electric, one manual)
 4 folding tables (wipeable surfaces), approximately 36" × 96"
14 stackable or foldable chairs
 1 floor-mounted kiln, electric (requires 220 volts and venting)
 2 deep utility sinks with approximately 12' countertops
 4 units utility shelving, 12" deep × 36" wide × 78" high

2 units utility shelving, 18" deep × 36" wide × 78" high

SPACE AND FINISH REQUIREMENTS:

300 square feet allotted in floor plan as possible area for curing and drying of green wares with lockable door and adjustable shelving
Countertop with overhead and base cabinets
Self-covered vinyl sheet flooring with heat-welded seams
Plastic laminate surfacing on all cabinets
Room should have adjacency to janitor's closet (with mop sink)
Cheerful but neutral colors
Wipeable window coverings
Medium-value finish colors, to reduce dust and spillage visibility

AESTHETIC REQUIREMENTS. Similar to functional programming, aesthetic programming is critical to the design of a space. How space (or an object within it) looks and feels communicates the aesthetic quality desired by the designer. In the sample room program for a pottery/ crafts room, comments such as "owner requests colors cheerful, but neutral" or "choose medium-value finish colors" are key phrases to assist in further selection of materials to appeal aesthetically to the target market.

When discussing a facility's desired aesthetic qualities, the initial approach should be general, allowing specific design features to fall into place later during the creative process. For example, the owner/developer of a proposed facility in the desert Southwest might express his or her feelings for the project to the design team in this manner:

In this area of the country, we have harsh climatic extremes. Our days are usually blistering hot. The bright noonday sun is painfully harsh, yet our evenings are balmy and delightful. Most folks who live in this region are here because they love the climate and the subtle nuances of the desert. Colors here in our surroundings range from vivid to subtle. The time of day also changes the mood and feeling of the place.

People here are receptive to a desert, Southwestern theme, but, interestingly, do not want a Mexican theme. We have a rich history of local native cultures from which you might draw inspiration. Geography may also be a good theme.

Many new developments in the area are using extremely bright colors. We will likely want to use them sparingly. Our goal is toward an indigenous look that is more timeless.

We have a fondness here for the interaction of indoor and outdoor space. In a design sense, we will want the spaces to flow together. In a real sense, we want one area to open out onto another area for early morning and evening use. We want our facility to have a very welcoming, "grand hotel" feeling for residents and their guests who come here.

This plainly spoken presentation contains a wealth of aesthetic clues for the architect and designer. These sorts of comments should be written and used in the same manner as functional programming. Ideally, this information should be included with the room-by-room functional-requirement breakdowns.

SUGGESTED READINGS

Design for Aging: An Architect's Guide. 1985. Washington, D.C.: AIA Press.
Reginier, V., and Pynoos, J. 1985. *Housing the Aged—Design Directives and Policy Considerations.* New York: Elsevier Science Publishing Co., Inc.

FREEDOM PLAZA, SUN CITY, ARIZONA

LEFT: A jade green balustrade capped with whitewashed oak complements the architecture of the lobby atrium and form a visual "halo" around a spacious lounge area. (Architecture: Freedom Group Inc.; interiors: Merlino Interior Design Associates; photo: James Cowlin.)

WESTLAKE VILLAGE, WESTLAKE, OHIO

RIGHT: Dark woodwork is enlivened by floral fabric on the stools and chairs in the billiard room. (Architecture: Shepard, Legan, Aldrian, Ltd.; interiors: Norman Harvey Associates, Inc./Jean-Lee Design, Inc.; billiard table: Playmaster Renaissance; bar stools, armchairs: Shelby Williams with Brunschwig & Fils fabric; photo: Robert W. Shimer/Hedrich Blessing.)

DESIGNING RETIREMENT FACILITIES

Housing that is adaptable to individual needs is especially important for those who become more frail as they age. Planners, developers, and design professionals must empathize with the individual older adults who will experience life in the setting that the planning and design professionals create. Project consultants should determine the appropriateness of their solutions in context to the older adult resident population being served. It is important for the design professional to project, from an end user's experiential point of view, what it will be like to walk through a space. How will the space feel? What will it look like? Will it be an emotionally satisfying experience?

While a group of individuals in a retirement home may share a similar disability, any given disability is likely to be present in varying degrees. Moreover, individual personal characteristics can affect functional ability levels. For slightly more cost, *adaptable housing* can ensure accessible housing that gives residents choice and flexibility according to their needs.

Traditionally, retirement housing has been designed to cater to the severely disabled, resulting in overdesign and unnecessary costs for those less physically disabled. Adaptable housing takes a middle-ground position—built-in contingency provisions for the severely disabled are accounted for, while the primary design thrust is appealing to those without significant impairment. Niche markets, such as assisted living, also allow for custom-suited residential units for various levels of impairment, with fixed costs appropriate for the niche market.

KEY ROOM-BY-ROOM ISSUES

When programming spaces on a room-by-room basis, the following issues should be considered:

ARCHITECTURAL DETAILING. The focus of architectural detailing involves both functional and aesthetic aspects of how the space will appear when constructed. Issues demanding consideration include the use of space, divisions of space, penetrations of space for doors, windows, decorative detailing, built-in features, cabinetry, and closets, floor-level changes, moldings, balconies, arches, and so on.

LIGHTING. Lighting affects not only what we see, but how we see it. When considering lighting requirements for space programming, it is important to understand the distinction between *essential lighting requirements* (task lighting) and *aesthetic lighting requirements* (decorative

**NEWPORT BAY
CONDOMINIUMS,
INDIANAPOLIS, INDIANA**

In the lobby, bright colors, new materials, and lots of natural light update a traditional style. (Architecture: Wolner Associates; interiors: Eden Design Associates; carpet: Devonshire Carpet; floor tiles: Fiandre; vinyl wallcovering: MDC, BFG; countertop: Formica; photo: Dan Francis, Mardan Photography.)

and mood-enhancing lighting). Most nondesign professionals do not understand these subtleties, so it is important to have good communication throughout the project team, and to be as specific as possible when specifying lighting needs. This information is useful in facility planning for functionality and flexibility issues.

BUILT-IN FEATURES. A wide variety of built-in features must be addressed in programming. The project philosophy is essential to the design team and must be articulated during the programming

stage by the owner/developer, in conjunction with the management and operations staff, to specify requirements regarding built-in furniture, fixtures, equipment, appliances, shelving, and so forth. Some owner/developers prefer that only the bare essentials, such as sink counters, closets, and vanities, be built-in, with all other furnishings being moveable; others prefer the opposite, wanting everything possible to be built-in. These scenarios have their respective pros and cons, but either way, the design team should be sufficiently flexible to conform to the owner's desire.

Discussion of function, style, edging on countertops, drawers, and doors, and hardware should also be articulated. The owner/developer should also determine whether architecture or interior design will handle the drawings and specifications of these items.

FINISH MATERIALS. Fixed architectural finish materials should be selected with an eye toward longevity, appropriateness of use, and the functional needs of residents who will be surrounded by them. For example, small ceramic tile, while being a useful and valid finish material, was used on every conceivable surface in the 1960s, with little thought given to appropriateness of location, style, longevity, and use. Today, we find exterior building veneers of this material peeling under extreme heat and cold; we find wall and floor surfaces covered with this ceramic tile experiencing extreme acoustics problems; we find wet areas where calcium deposits and fungus growth are problematic; we find areas where color selection for such a permanent material now seems overly bold or garish; and, as a result, we find current design professionals severely criticizing the original designers who selected these treatments.

Fixed-finish materials include doors, walls, ceilings, floors, toilet partitions, lockers, window frames, baseboards, handrails, sinks, toilets, shower stalls, millwork, lighting fixtures, signage, exterior fascia, window glazing, hardware, and so forth. These materials become fixed real estate (as opposed to moveable furnishings), and therefore must be selected with maintenance, durability, appearance, longevity, and flexibility over the lifetime of the building in mind.

THE GATESWORTH
AT ONE McKNIGHT PLACE,
ST. LOUIS, MISSOURI

The garden dining room connects the spa and indoor swimming pool through an interior courtyard at the right. The dining chair fabric is laminated for easy cleaning. (Architecture: Arthur J. Sitzwohl & Associates; interiors: LVK Associates; dining chairs: Chairmasters; loveseats: Brown Jordan; tables: Berco; upholstery: Duralee, DesignTex; carpet: Design Weave; wallcovering: Vicrtex, Schumacher & Co.; ceiling: Armstrong; photo: Alise O'Brien.)

ACOUSTICS. Acoustics is an often-ignored area of programming. Most people understand the importance of good acoustics but rarely understand how to achieve them. The design team should determine, early in the planning stage, the areas where good acoustics are most essential. With older adults, particularly in public areas, good acoustics can be achieved by various means, including applied finish materials and architectural detailing (baffling, penetrations, absorption, screening, or reflecting) amplifying, and masking.

SAFETY AND CODES. It is the responsibility of each consultant to design and specify solutions that meet local guidelines for sanitation, safety, flammability, toxicity, seismic safety, lighting, accessibility, energy consumption, and other applicable factors. Developers, management, and operating staff should advise the design consultants of any unique or peculiar local codes. Code requirements should not be taken lightly—there have been several unfortunate projects where consultants unfamiliar with local codes

(or owners who chose to ignore them) were required to make major facility alterations in order to secure a certificate of occupancy or licensure. Local inspection agencies are generally unyielding in areas of public health and safety, and with good reason.

Specific areas of code-related concern include building structure, site drainage, building set-backs, air circulation, electrical loads, fire-suppression systems, exhaust systems, load-bearing capacity of floors, exit locations, exit widths and heights, lighting levels, sewage and trash handling, handrail and grab bar heights, handicapped access to all basic services, sanitation and toxicity of finish materials, stability of design features under seismic stress, safety of floor-level changes, space allotment per capita, infection control, safety of moveable equipment and furnishings, and much more. Clearly, everyone must do their homework.

FLEXIBILITY. Flexibility within a facility is more an issue of convenience in service delivery than of necessity. How flexible a facility is, however, can later

THE ROSSMOOR REGENCY,
LAGUNA BEACH,
CALIFORNIA

A favorite spot to socialize and listen to music is the lounge, which is separated from the lobby by a half-wall of plantings. Limited-edition Italian prints adorn the walls. (Architecture: Arthur J. Sitzwohl & Associates; interiors: LVK Associates; large area rug: Carpets from London; drapery fabric: Scalamandre; tables: Lane; lamps: Remington; club chairs and sofas: A. Rudin; end tables, consoles: Emerson et Cie; photo: Milroy/McAleer.)

THE HEARTWOOD, TACOMA, WASHINGTON

The family room doubles as a chapel. (Architecture: Merritt & Pardini; interiors: Hendrix Interiors; carpet: Atlas; window treatments: Verosol Pleated Shades; furniture: Thomasville with fabric by Robert Allen Fabrics; lamps: Stiffel; stained glass: Mansion Glass of Olympia; photo: Mark Ricketts Photography.)

affect its ability to expand its physical structure and deliver new services to residents.

Flexibility tends to be intangible, and planning for it can affect how residents and staff will accomplish the tasks of daily living and daily work. In general, a little extra forethought in consideration of future needs during programming, design, and even construction will enhance the long-term cost-effectiveness of the design. While planning the space, the development team should note, in writing, conditions for future use, and plan accordingly.

MAINTENANCE. Facilities, much like people, undergo an aging process, a slow deterioration that starts to occur with the completion of a facility, or even with the beginning of construction. This deterioration, which is due to natural elements and normal wear from use, has an obvious effect on a facility's longevity. With this in mind, the development team should plan for both ease of maintenance and maintenance-free solutions.

Very few materials are truly maintenance-free, but some require far less maintenance than others. Thoughtful design detailing can make the difference between a piece of furniture or an architectural detail being a cleaning nightmare and an element that is easy to maintain. How the material will wear is another important consideration—cleaning itself exerts wear and stress on a finish. What chemicals, abrasion, or heat will be used? How often will cleaning be necessary? What is the typical life and cost of a given material? How easy and costly is it to replace? How much staff will be required to maintain it? Are there more costly yet less labor-intensive materials or methods available to do the job? All of these concerns must be weighed. The real question for the designer is, "What are the real operational costs for maintaining the functional and aesthetic requirements of the building?" The answer(s) will ultimately affect the bottom line of the facility. Special criteria for maintenance issues should be noted in programming notes.

BUDGET. Just as maintenance concerns affect yearly operational budgets, initial expenditures on mortar, bricks, equipment, and furnishings affect capital improvement and capital equipment budgets. All project consultants should be able to offer the owner/developer several options on each issue affecting construction and future operational costs.

The design community has come to regard the term *custom-designed* with skepticism. As a result, many owner/operators accept (or even demand) "stock" solutions, straight from the manufacturer's standard assembly line, with no thought toward suitability, proven performance, or cost. Furniture, fixtures, or equipment manufacturers often charge unreasonable amounts, or "what the market will bear," simply because they are the only ones producing given items. Wary owners and operators should shop around to satisfy themselves that the best solutions have been offered and for the best value. A "custom" piece of furniture often can be designed and built at a fraction of the cost of a "stock" piece, and may perform better.

As a simple example of this, consider a certain conference table, which was required to have a fold-away top for more compact storage. The manufacturer of this stock item, thanks to a "unique" mechanism that costs a mere fraction of the total cost of the table to produce, charged three times the normal retail value for a table. When the market realized that a similar solution could be "custom"-produced at a fraction of the cost of the stock item, the manufacturer lost business. The lesson here is that stock solutions are not always the least expensive or the best. Developers should challenge consultants to locate, or create, and demonstrate the best-value solutions. This pertains to furnishings, moveable equipment, building finishes, mechanical, electrical, and plumbing systems, structural design, foodservice equipment, laundry equipment, and more.

MOVABLE FURNISHINGS. Owner-provided criteria for moveable furnishings is necessary for consultants to move forward on a project. The capacity of a room and the type and quantity of pieces required within it are necessary. A shopping list of furniture and equipment requirements for a given space enables both architect and designer to lay out workable solutions for resident activities within that space. Issues of storage, circulation, flexibility, multifunctional use, and maximum capacity can be determined with this information.

Special criteria for furnishings pieces should be noted. For example, the programming criteria on a dining chair might be:

- Must sit comfortably for long periods of time
- Seat depth must not be too deep
- Must be normal dining height
- Must sit firmly
- Seat back must give good lumbar support
- Must have arms that fit under table top
- Arms must not extend further than ¾ length of chair
- Arms must be padded and provide good user leverage support
- Upholstery covering must be patterned to camouflage wear
- Upholstery cover must repel moisture and staining; detailing must attract or hide food crumbs or odors
- Upholstery filling and cover must be flameproof
- Upholstery must be on-site-recoverable by maintenance staff
- Frame must have wood finish and traditional French styling
- Must be lightweight and moveable by residents
- Must be extremely stable from tipping hazards
- Must have carpet glides/no casters
- Must fit in a budget range of $185 to $225

This is just one example of the detailed specifics that programming requirements can denote for individual furnishings items. The more information an owner/operator can give to the design team, the easier it will be to fulfill levels of expectation.

DESIGNING FOR AGING IN PLACE

As the seniors population moves through the various stages of step-down care, the design community must realize the need for individuals to be uprooted as little as possible from their existing residences during the normal aging process, which may include both physical and mental constraints. This is known as *aging in place*. The driving factor of designing for aging in place is for the social and emotional well-being of the residents—when an individual ages, it is important to maintain consistency and familiarity with established routines and social patterns. These issues of familiarity and consistency are vital to a person's sense of independence and socialization, and concern for the aging-in-place phenomenon is critical for effective seniors design.

Since aging in place involves ongoing familiarity with personal space and belongings, physical acuities can be overcome by thoughtful and adaptable design solutions. These solutions are generally preplanned years in advance of anticipated need. Planning and design schemes should be geared toward solutions for *future* need, not just toward adequate solutions for current demands.

To design a space for maximum flexibility for the aging individual, an overall design philosophy must prevail. For example, planners must learn to think reflexively about all solutions existing on two height levels—one for normal living and standard heights, the other at a lower height for wheelchair-bound individuals. Some design specifics that can aid planners in the process of designing for aging in place include the following:

SPACE ALLOWANCES AND ACCESS. The space allocations within existing congregate living units are often adequate for wheelchair-bound individuals or for those who use walking aids. The key space issue here is allowing for adequate passage and turn-around.

One problem involves the widths of doorways and passageways. While many facilities currently have doorways 30 inches (76 cm) wide leading into resident units, 32 inches (81 cm) is recommended for doors, and 36 to 48 inches (91 to 122 cm) is recommended for access to all private areas through which a wheelchair will pass. This applies not only to entranceways and interior doorways, but also to bedrooms, bathrooms, kitchens, living rooms, and so on.

The wheelchair-bound resident's space requirements are dictated by the space required to move about in a wheelchair. A standard wheelchair requires a resting space of 10 square feet (1 square meter), or 30 by 48 inches (76 by 122 cm), and a turning radius of 60 inches (152 cm). When designing small, confined spaces, such as kitchens, bathrooms, vestibules, and so forth, allowing for the proper turning radius is crucial, in terms of both comfort for the individual and avoiding damage to the surrounding walls, doorways, doors, and cabinets.

Most spaces designed for aging in place allow more open space, anticipating the future possibilities of wheelchairs and walking aids. Some argue that space allowances for the wheelchair-bound need not be any larger than normal space allotments, suggesting that how the space is *configured* is what really matters; others argue that, in the long run, developers are best advised to provide the extra space. Two simple factors favor the latter position: First, increased space allows the handicapped individual more freedom of movement to accomplish the normal tasks of daily living; second, it reduces the risk of damage to the building itself.

ELEVATORS AND RAMPS. Floor-level changes should be avoided in seniors facilities. Any necessary ramps should be planned and included during the initial construction of the facility. Ramps should have no more than one foot (30 cm) of rise per 20 feet (6 meters) of distance, with landings (preferably including benches) at every 40 feet (12 meters). Handrails should be located on both sides of ramps and stairs. Stairs should be at least 4 feet (122 cm) wide, and ramps should be at least 5 feet (152 cm)

THE HEARTWOOD,
TACOMA, WASHINGTON

The waiting lounge, where residents watch for the arrival of visitors, features colorful artwork and an abundance of plants "to bring the outside in," says designer Liz Hendrix. (Architecture: Merritt & Pardini; interiors: Hendrix Interiors; chairs: Brandrud with fabric by Robert Allen; tables: Custom by Briarwood Furniture; sconces: Lightolier; torchiere: Stiffel; artwork: Design Source; carpet: Atlas; photo: Mark Ricketts Photography.)

HEATHERWOOD AT
KINGS WAY, YARMOUTH,
MASSACHUSETTS

Floral fabrics, light pine
furnishings, and awning-striped
wallpaper in the lounge are
reminiscent of a summer beach
house. (Architecture: Woo &
Williams, Hammer, Kiefer & Todd;
interiors: Design 1 Interiors; bar
stools, tables: Jenson Custom
furniture; chairs: Shelby Williams;
carpet: Milliken; wallcovering:
Columbus Coated Fabrics; photo:
Cymie Payne.)

wide—enough to allow two wheelchair-bound individuals to pass in opposite directions.

Elevators should have sufficient door widths to allow the comfortable passage of wheelchairs and gurneys, with turning radius as the prevailing factor. Elevator cabs should be at least 5 feet (152 cm) deep by 6½ feet (198 cm) long, and should be able to comfortably carry two or three individuals standing along with a wheelchair-bound individual. Elevator doors should close more slowly than normal and pause immediately after the door-closing sequence begins. Elevator buttons should have simple messages in oversized letters and numbers. These buttons and controls should be located no higher than 48 inches (122 cm). Audible tones should mark the elevator's arrival at each floor, and tactile or braille messages should be included in the graphics near the elevator controls. Handrails should be provided in elevator cabs, and, if possible, a bench should also be provided. Entry thresholds should be as smooth and level as possible, with no more than a half-inch (1.3-cm) rise.

HANDRAILS, CRASH RAILS, AND GRAB BARS. In many new retirement facilities, such design details as handrails, crash rails, and grab bars are often viewed as negative features that reinforce old notions about the frail elderly. Nonetheless, local codes require handrails in many locations, regardless of the age of the facility's users, and stairs and ramps are logical locations for such safety features. However, to design for the future needs of an aging population, certain details and advance planning can make the aging process smoother and less problematic. Blocking can be built into walls of bathrooms, corridors, hallways, and any other areas that may later need handrails or grab bars. This low-cost measure, which can be added while a building is initially under construction, may sit dormant behind walls for years until it is needed to mount handrails or grab bars. The handrails should be mounted 32 inches (81 cm) above the finished floor.

Grab bars are useful in wet areas—bathrooms, pool and spa areas, bathing rooms, and so forth. Residents will often use a grab bar for leverage while getting out of a bathtub or shower. These should be mounted horizontally. Specific placement will vary according to space configuration and resident needs, but an abundance of blocking in the walls will guarantee the necessary flexibility to meet individual residents' requirements.

Handrails and grab bars should be no larger than an inch and a half (3.8 cm) and no less than an inch (2.5 cm) wide. While the type of material may vary, it should in any case be smooth and free of splinters or sharp edges. If available and affordable, hardwood or nylon handrails and grab bars are less cold to the touch and less institutional-looking, and can be treated with many finishes and colors. Wood also lends itself to a variety of profiles, which can complement a facility's decor nicely.

CABINETRY. The main features of cabinetry for aging in place should be modularity and adjustability. Cabinets built in standard module widths of 32 or 16 inches (81 or 41 cm) can later be rearranged or removed to allow undercounter access of a stool or wheelchair. While normal cabinetry has a typical toekick or base of 4 inches (10 cm), an 8-inch (20-cm) toekick or base built in two equal layers provides more flexibility for height adjustment—one layer can be removed, lowering the entire cabinet and countertop, to meet the needs of those requiring a lower countertop height. Cubic storage

capacity is reduced by this feature, but the overall increase in flexibility, which can be used as a selling feature, is worthwhile.

Because people are not all the same height, there is no one countertop height that ideally meets the needs of all residents for all tasks. Preferred countertop heights range from 26 to 36 inches (66 to 91 cm). A satisfactory compromise for most individuals is 32 inches (81 cm), which also works for the mounting of sinks and lavatories. For the sight-impaired, place a contrasting band of surfacing material on the leading edge of the countertop.

Removing cabinet door fronts or using sliding cabinet doors often help wheelchair-bound individuals access stored items; lazy Susans, sliding shelves, retractable baskets, and extra drawers are also helpful. Most wheelchair users have difficulty reaching onto or into shelves that are mounted higher than 47 inches (119 cm) or lower than 9 inches (23 cm) from the floor; a height of 18 inches (46 cm) is easily reachable by most individuals.

Cabinet modules beneath sinks should be removable, to allow access by those seated on a stool or in a wheelchair. A shallower sink should be selected initially, to allow a clear 26-inch (66-cm) height to bottom of sink for leg clearance. Kitchens laid out in L- or U-shaped configurations are easier for the

wheelchair-bound to negotiate, and are preferred to straight galley layouts. It is important that clearance in kitchen aisles between cabinets be no less than 42 inches (107 cm). Ovens with side-hinged doors mounted at counter height are ideal for wheelchair access, and an undercounter space beneath the oven also makes access easier.

The strength required to open cabinet doors should be considered—magnetic catch mechanisms with zero-resistance hinges are best. A few manufacturers are now producing cabinetry for aging-in-place flexibility, so designers should be aware of new products.

APPLIANCES. Appliances with larger-than-normal dials and buttons are helpful for those with impaired sight and/or manual dexterity, and large, high-contrast print on dials and instructional areas is helpful for the sight-impaired. Stoves or range tops should have dials and control knobs positioned up front, avoiding the need to reach over a hot pan or burner to adjust the heat. Many manufacturers are now producing appliances that automatically turn themselves off, such as stoves, ovens and irons, and these are worth investigating as well.

BATHROOMS. Bathrooms that can accommodate aging in place can be constructed within the typical space constraints of most housing projects if

THE ROSSMOOR REGENCY, LAGUNA BEACH, CALIFORNIA

The bathroom features single-handle antiscald faucets, high-seat toilets, shower doors that fold for easy access, and seats in the bathtubs. Wallpaper is an optional extra. (Architecture: Terry Architects; interiors: Jung Designs; faucets: Delta; bathtubs: Kimstock; counters: Corian; sink: American Standard; photo: Milroy/McAleer.)

the entry door is mounted on the long wall (not the short wall, as is typical). The bathroom door should open outward (rather than inward, as is also typical). Fixtures must allow adequate turn-around space for wheelchairs. Toilet seats should be 19 inches (48 cm) high, with side-mounted grab bars projecting beyond the front of the toilet by at least 6 inches (15 cm). Toilet stall areas in public bathrooms should have clear 48-inch-square (122-cm-square) single horizontal grab bars mounted 32 inches (81 cm) high on both sides. A relatively inexpensive grab bar or leverage point can be designed for residential bathrooms by designing a weight-bearing sink/countertop to wrap around the toilet.

Although many residents prefer bathtubs to showers, bathtub sidewalls present tripping and slipping hazards. If bathtubs are provided, include a built-in deck or ledge at one end of the tub, on which bathers can sit and pivot while lifting their legs over the sidewall.

For shower users, a stable bench or portable shower seat is important. Water faucets should be mounted on the sidewall, not on the end wall of the bathing area. Hand-held shower spray units are helpful, as are shower heads on articulating arms, which can be adjusted to the heights of various users. Bathroom floors can be gradually sloped at the shower area to avoid having a curb wall, eliminating the hazard of tripping and facilitating wheelchair access.

Grab bars must be located according to the needs of each individual. Horizontal grab bars generally offer the best access. Bathtub areas should include one grab bar mounted 9 inches (23 cm) above the tub rim and a second grab bar mounted 32 inches (81 cm) above the tub rim. Each bar should be at least 24 inches (61 cm) long, ideally running the full length of the bathing area. Sinks and countertops should be 32 inches (81 cm) high, with undersink wheelchair access. Mirrors may need to be mounted with a slight forward tilt, to aid shorter or wheelchair-bound residents. Flooring surfaces should be slip-resistant and contiguous with shower-floor surfaces.

SWITCHES AND OUTLETS. Electrical switches should be mounted 48 inches (122 cm) above the finished floor; wall

CLASSIC RESIDENCE
BY HYATT,
TEANECK, NEW JERSEY

The mailroom lounge is spare but inviting, with a French country flavor. (Architecture: Fusco, Shaffer & Pappas, Inc.; interiors: Culpepper, McAuliffe and Meaders, Inc.; carpet: Trafford Park Carpets; seating: Custom Craft, Hospitality Furniture Company, Shelby Williams; fabric: Donghia, Payne Fabric, Brunschwig & Fils; tables: Kreiss, Murray's Iron Works; shutters, drapery: Unlimited Design Resources; chandelier: Alger Lighting; photo: Gabriel Benzur.)

THE RENAISSANCE,
SHERMAN, TEXAS

Generous window walls let
passersby see who is in the card
room. (Architecture: Archon;
interiors: ABV & Associates;
photo: Peter Paige.)

outlets, including outlets for electricity, central vacuum systems, television antennae, and cable and telephone jacks, should be 15 inches (38 cm) above the floor.

THRESHOLDS. Flooring transitions should be no greater than half an inch (1.3 cm), to accommodate wheeled conveyances, shuffling feet, and walking aids. Transitions from one type of flooring material to another must be smooth and as level as possible. Thresholds should be avoided whenever possible; when they are unavoidable, their edges should be beveled, not sharp or abrupt.

SIGHT AND HEARING. Telephone ringers, alarm bells and doorbells should be loud enough for those with hearing impairments to hear them adequately. A visual signal can help notify those who are deaf of normal messages or dangers and vibrating annunciators can help to

inform the profoundly sight- and hearing-impaired along these same lines.

Highly polished finish surfaces should be avoided, as they distract individuals who have problems with contrast and glare. Mirrored surfaces, which can be confusing for those with poor vision and depth perception, should be avoided as well.

MAILBOXES AND WALL-MOUNTED TELEPHONES. These necessities should be mounted no higher than 54 inches (137 cm) above the floor; most residents in wheelchairs find that 48 inches (122 cm) is an ideal height for these items.

TRAVEL DISTANCES AND RESTING. Corridors should be broken up with design features and resting places for residents. Three hundred feet (91 meters) is the maximum distance a senior can be expected to walk in a comfortable

amount of time. Attractive benches, built-in or moveable, may be used for rest and carrying on conversation, encouraging the step-down socialization process. These features should be straightforward and recognizable, to help those who have difficulty orienting themselves to their environment but are still mobile. Contrast, symbols and color differentiation can help create distinctive, memorable orientation points. Similarity in floor designs and in architectural and design detailing may save initial construction costs, but may also require additional expense in terms of labor and redesign in the long term.

SIGNAGE. The key to wayfinding is signage. The needs of older adults, especially those over 80, accentuate the need for well-conceived, easy-to-read signage at frequent junctures, not only for convenience but for safety reasons as well. Messages should be logical, simple, and clear. Lettering should be uncomplicated, bold, and high in contrast. Signage symbols should be simple and

easily translatable, especially for those who are cognitively impaired. Tactile messages may also be necessary for the sight-impaired.

To summarize, the types of facilities for seniors are varied and overlapping in characteristics; therefore, it is impossible to list the thousands of specific solutions possible in a retirement project. However, the *principles* around which a team of planners forms solutions for senior residential needs are consistent—they revolve around the physiological and psychological needs of the older adult market segment as user. Design for aging affects the entire population, not just the aged. Therefore, it should be good design for all ages.

SUGGESTED READINGS

Brukoff, B. 1989. Manifesto: Against Cerebral Design. *Designer's West*. August: 166.

Valins, M. 1988. *Housing for Elderly People*. London: The Architectural Press.

FORWOOD MANOR, WILMINGTON, DELAWARE

The living room is located just behind the lobby. Light from the courtyard below flows into the living room from curtainless French doors. (Architecture: Moeckel Carbonell Associates; interiors; Interior Design Associates; photo: Tom Crane.)

CHAPTER SEVEN

SOCIAL CONSIDERATIONS IN AGING

NEWPORT BAY
CONDOMINIUMS,
INDIANAPOLIS, INDIANA

The atrium is meant to suggest
the feeling of an outdoor park
with adjacent streetscapes.
(Architecture: Wolner Associates,
interiors: Eden Design Associates;
carpet: Bentley, Richmond; ceramic
wall tiles: Gail Architectural
Ceramics; paint: Benjamin Moore;
light post: Georgian Art-lighting
Designs; Seating: Country Casual
with fabric by Lazarus Fabrics;
floor tiles: Fiandre; photo: Dan
Francis, Mardan Photography.)

A SOCIAL PERSPECTIVE

There are several traditional theories of aging, which represent knowledgeable people's views on what they think the aging process entails. More recently, new theories in the social aspects of aging have been offered, somewhat countering the traditional, and somewhat negative, theories.

Our images of aging are learned from and continuously reinforced in the media. As Ken Dychtwald (1989) has noted, "At least in part, our images of aging are negative because of our glorification of youth. The image of youth as vigorous and powerful and sexy has as its shadow an image of older people as incompetent, inflexible, wedded to the past, desexed, uncreative, poor, sick, and slow."

Indeed, age is one of many criteria for determining the position of individuals in society. *Age stratification* is the term used to describe this phenomenon, and because aging is experienced and re-acted to differently in different societies, all societies can be characterized accord-ing to their relative degree of age strati-fication. For the purposes of this text, we will describe the aging process as it ex-ists in the United States, beginning with a review of the leading theories.

Taking the most recent first, David Wolfe's 1990 *ageless theory* is a blending of Wolfe's own ideas, psychologist Abraham Maslow's hierarchy of needs, and psy-chologist Erik Erikson's stages of person-ality development. Wolfe, a consumer behavior specialist, approaches aging from a consumer-behavior perspective, and suggests that many of the traditional theories suggesting that older people are inherently withdrawn, disengaged, ex-cluded, and the like are biased and condescending.

Wolfe describes three experiential stages of life development: *the possession experience years, the catered experience years,* and *the being experience years.* During the possession experience years, a person is intent on accumulating material and ani-mate things. Examples include first cars, a first home, furniture, a first significant other, a spouse, a pet, a baby, and so forth. During the catered experience years, the adult seeks services—travel, entertainment, upscale dining, and so forth—rather than things. While Wolfe hesitates to assign age brackets to his life periods, he suggests that we enter our catered experience years around our 40s or so, and that this stage wanes in the late 40s and middle 50s. During the be-ing experience years, to which Wolfe dedicates his major effort, a person be-gins to explore life's meanings, becomes spiritual and outwardly focused, and seeks to satisfy personal-growth needs.

This closely parallels Erikson's eighth personality stage (wisdom) and Maslow's fifth and highest state (self-actualization). Overall, Wolfe translates these predecessors' theories in a modern, consumer-oriented context; specifically, he addresses how business marketing products and services can best position their products to appeal to older adults.

Moving backward to the 1960s, we tend to find more negative theories in aging, which in large part reflect the eras in which they were developed. Among the more positive of the negative theories is Roman and Taietz's *activity theory*, which posits social integration, socialization, and recreation as primary factors. This theory suggests that as people age, they will continue to behave as they did in their earlier years. For example, people who are active, remain active. Because the theory holds that people will be happier if they are active, it supports the establishment of a recreation or activities director in a traditional long-term care setting. Unfortunately, not everyone can live up to the theory's lofty goals. "Indeed, by suggesting that the aged 'ought' to remain active to age successfully, [the activity theory] places people who are not or cannot remain active in an awkward position, implying that they are failures" (Ward 1984). In short, the activity theory ignores declining health among the aged, especially for those 80 or more years of age.

The *developmental* or *life-cycle theory* suggests that aging human beings are like objects in an expanding universe—the unique traits we each possess become more unique and differentiated. As we age, the theory holds, we no longer

ST. CATHERINE'S VILLAGE, MADISON, MISSISSIPPI

TOP: In the Natatorium, residents can sit in the whirlpool and enjoy a lake view. The swimming pool is wheelchair-accessible. (Architecture and interiors: Cooke Douglass Farr, Ltd.; tile: American Olean; lighting: Lithonia; benches: Mae Martin; tables, chairs: Grosfillex; photo: John O'Hagan.)

BOTTOM: Bordering the dining area, slate is used in the corridor that accesses and runs parallel to the courtyard. This skid-resistant material is also used in foyers and other areas that connect to the outside. The carpeted corridor leads to the assisted living facility. (Architecture and interiors: Cooke Douglass Farr, Ltd.; slate: Tatko Slate Company; carpet: Shaw Industries; paint: Benjamin Moore; light fixtures: Kurt Versen; photo: John O'Hagan.)

FAIRWAYS AT BROOKLINE
VILLAGE, STATE COLLEGE,
PENNSYLVANIA

The guest dining room on the
ground floor provides an ideal
spot for small parties or for
families to dine in privacy.
(Architecture: Robert L. Beers,
AIA, Architects; interiors: Merlino
Interior Design Associates;
carpet: Couristan; chairs: Barrit;
photo: Richard Quindry.)

have the strong need to belong to groups that we had in our teens and we tend to become more individualistic. As aging progresses, enlightened individuals develop their own standards of behavior and are less motivated by societal mores. Individualism becomes more extreme and the center of who we were diminishes. As critics have pointed out, however, what the theory refers to as individuality can all too easily be mistaken for selfishness. For example, in a classic life-cycle theory scenario, an elderly gentleman, shortly after arriving at a party, puts on his hat and says to his wife, "Mama, let's go home." When informed that the party had just begun, he says, "When I was younger, I had to try to please many people so that I could succeed. Now that I'm retired, I do whatever I damn well want to do."

The *societal disengagement theory* developed by Cumming and Henry in the early 1960s emanates from mortality, suggesting that there must be an orderly transition from older to younger members of society. Since older individuals have a greater probability of dying, a smooth-functioning society tends to want to depend more on its younger (i.e. safer) members. The effect on seniors is

obvious—not feeling needed, they see themselves as societal outcasts and, therefore, disengage.

Another view of aging, a social view, is the *birth cohort theory*, which posits that individuals are molded by experiences they share with others in their age group. "Society can be thought of as composed of a succession of cohorts flowing through time, each of which is shaped by a unique configuration of events. . . . The shared experience of a cohort will shape the norms, values, attitudes, and behaviors of its members" (Ward 1984). For example, people who lived through the Great Depression have a particular perspective of the world; baby-boomers, during whose childhoods there was tremendous economic and technological expansion and explosive social changes, have a different perspective. Indeed, we are a function of our environment, this theory holds. Understanding birth cohort theory and, more specifically, *cohort-centrism*, under which different birth cohorts view identical phenomena in distinctive ways, contributes to a comprehensive understanding of older adults.

Robert Atchley's successive *phases of retirement*—preretirement, honeymoon,

disenchantment, reorientation, stability, and termination—offer thoughts on developing senior housing. In short, Atchley believes seniors exercise their option to seek changes during the preretirement/honeymoon phase and the disenchantment/reorientation phase. The former period might be characterized by a move to the Sunbelt, the latter by a move back to one's original geographic area, suggesting that prospective owner/developers should conduct studies to determine the phase or phases of the different market segments in the primary market area.

SENIOR LIVING TRENDS FOR THE 1990s

The design of retirement facilities may change significantly in the near future. As changing societal trends affect social programs, and as technology and architectural fashions affect physical structures, planners, architects, and designers must be ready to keep up with future developments on all fronts.

Insight gained from a study of a local market can pinpoint the services and products the given market demands.

MAYFLOWER RETIREMENT COMMUNITY, WINTER PARK, FLORIDA

ABOVE: The Mayflower "is a contemporary interpretation of the Spanish Mission architecture prevalent in the area," says Fugleberg Koch project manager Jim McCabe. Synthetic stucco surfacing and metal tile–like roofing translate the look to the two six-story residential towers. The independent living facility's amenities, such as screened-in porches, generous walking paths, and adjacent golf course, focus activities on the outdoors. (Architecture: Fugleberg Koch Architects, Inc.; interiors: Design Collective, Inc., in association with Spaces Inc.; photo: Philip Eschbach.)

TOP RIGHT: The facility's dining room takes on the look of an upscale restaurant. Each apartment is equipped with a kitchen, so "guests should feel like the meals they eat here are just like dining out," says interior designer Lauren Shapiro. More formal than the Mayflower's other spaces, the room features bleached wood chairs, colorful fabrics in Monet-inspired tones, and original artwork by local artists. (Architecture: Fugleberg Koch Architects, Inc.; interiors: Design Collective, Inc., in association with Spaces Inc.; chairs, banquettes: Shelby Williams with DesignTex fabric; carpet: Stratton; valences: Suncraft Draperies;

paint: Benjamin Moore; art: Jean Schubert; china: Lenox; flatware: Oneida Silversmiths; glassware: Libbey; napery: Quip Linens; photo: Philip Eschbach.)

BOTTOM RIGHT: The private dining room makes use of reproduction furnishings, including a china cabinet. (Architecture: Fugleberg Koch Architects, Inc.; interiors: Design Collective, Inc., in association with Spaces Inc.; table: Myrtle Desk; chairs, upholstery: St. Timothy Chairs; china cabinet: Councill Companies; draperies, blinds: Suncraft Draperies; carpet: J&J Industries; art: Corporate Art Services; photo: Philip Eschbach.)

ST. CATHERINE'S VILLAGE, MADISON, MISSISSIPPI

LEFT: Slate and copper dress up the fireplace in the commons area. The reception desk is shown at left. (Architecture and interiors: Cooke Douglass Farr, Ltd.; slate: Tatko Slate Company; wallcovering: Maharam, F. Schumacher; carpet: Harbinger; paint: Benjamin Moore; light fixtures: Kurt Versen; couch, chairs: Wieland; upholstery fabric: Jack Lenor Larsen, F. Schumacher; occasional tables: Nucraft; photo: John O'Hagan.)

ABOVE: The 16-seat deli, a general store, and other activity areas adjoin the courtyard, creating the effect of a town square. (Architecture and interiors: Cooke Douglass Farr, Ltd.; tile: Iarkett, bar stools: Loewenstein; tables and chairs: Grosfillex; bar top: Formica; photo: John O'Hagan.)

Demand represents an opportunity, a need waiting to be satisfied; latent demand represents an unknown demand for products and services not yet identified. The right product and service mix, coupled with a perception of value, leads to a successful business.

A feasibility study conducted early in the conceptual phase must be weighed against actual development costs. The study should measure the preferences of a demographic profile of prospective buyers against their willingness and ability to pay for such preferences, which in turn will determine options for programs and other design amenities for the facility.

As America's seniors population has increased (and continues to do so), there has been (and will continue to be), a proliferation of retirement facilities targeted to various market segments. There has also been a gradual evolution of the actual definition of project types and of the offerings expected within these types. In each facility, it is important to program and design the structure for the ability level of the least capable prospective

resident. The trend, however, is to inspire and encourage residents to achieve greater levels of independence. The more independent the residents are, the fewer staff members are required to service the residents' needs, resulting in significant financial savings for the facility and residents alike. In addition, research suggests that more independent residents enjoy their environment to a greater extent.

Many owner/developers are hesitant to invest in the projected trends of the future, wary of fads that may become quickly outdated. And indeed, there must be clear distinctions made between a valid program and design trends and short-lived fads that quickly vanish from the scene.

During the past 20 years of retirement facility development, there have been a number of trends including changing attitudes toward aging, actual demographic data showing extended life expectancy through improved health care, and changing consumer demands for real estate products. Many trends accepted in the 1950s and 1960s are now

THE QUADRANGLE,
HAVERFORD,
PENNSYLVANIA

The commons lounge clusters comfortable seating in front of the fireplace. Built-in shelving displays antiques and collectibles. (Architecture: Wallace Roberts & Todd; interiors: Marriott Corporation; sofa: Sherrill with S. Harris fabric; wing chairs: Sherrill with Kravet fabric; tables: Weimann, Madison Square, LaBarge; lamps: Frederick Cooper; carpet: Milliken; photo: Matt Wargo.)

merely historical markers and reference points against which today's preferences are measured. While some of today's trends will undoubtedly suffer the same fate, the following issues are worthy of consideration by anyone thinking of developing a retirement facility.

INDEPENDENCE VS. DEPENDENCE. When designing a facility, the planning and design team should ask the following question: Will each seemingly trivial decision we make assist residents in becoming more dependent or independent? To answer this question effectively and meaningfully, it is imperative for planners and designers to view the task at hand through the eyes of a prospective resident. In order to encourage independence, residents should be urged and enabled to do as much for themselves as possible, including meal preparation (or getting to meal service), daily personal grooming, bathing, dressing, housekeeping, personal laundry, shopping, fitness activities, participation in social, recreational, and educational activities, and so forth. Each instance of a staff member being called for help in completing a task merely diminishes the individual's belief in his or her own abilities. Indeed, the more options available to us, the more we are in control of our own lives and the happier we are as individuals. The goal of many facilities, therefore, is to stimulate older adults to become their own agents of change.

Studies show that longevity is tied to having a reason to wake up and have something important to do and to look forward to. Two older women—attorneys in their late 70s who established their law practice after their husbands passed away—were interviewed on the television show *60 Minutes*. When the interviewer reminded one of the two women that she had once said she was going to retire at age 80, she replied, "I must have said that when I was 75!" While this clearly underscores her desire to feel needed, a bit of reading between the lines also reveals her unspoken thought: "When I stop working, I'll die!"

VOLUNTEERISM. A significant 1990s trend among older adults is toward increased volunteerism and committee participation. Seniors are often involved in volunteer activities to a greater extent than the population at large. While this may be true simply because retired people have more time, it is also true that seniors enjoy meaningful activities that allow them to help others (perhaps a manifestation of Wolfe's being experience years?). While some seniors prefer to enjoy a steady diet of leisure activities—we've all seen the bumper sticker that says, I'M SPENDING MY CHILDREN'S INHERITANCE—the majority of older adults serve in very important volunteer activities, including census and community health services, rape crisis and abuse counseling, hospice duties with AIDS and terminally ill patients, Planned Parenthood counseling, Humane Society services, vocational training, educational counseling, Red Cross and medical research efforts, crime-alert programs, youth outreach programs, literacy education, foster home services, alcohol and drug abuse counseling, meals-on-wheels programs, bilingual training programs, community arts services, and much more.

RESIDENTS ASSOCIATIONS. Executive directors of seniors campuses have begun to appreciate the value in the trend toward their facilities' social, educational, and recreational activities being organized and administered by residents associations. The benefits include residents exercising self-determination in creating an agenda for activities that interest them, the development of initiative in problem solving and organizing, the recognition of a need for interdependence, the development of social and leadership skills, and so forth.

DESIGN TRENDS FOR THE 1990s

COST. While there is a great range of options now available for seniors housing and care, many of these options remain financially unviable for a large number of low-income seniors, whose estates may consist primarily of meager Social Security or pension benefits. Various government programs and nonprofit organizations exist to help these seniors obtain affordable housing, but these resources, even if they help low-income seniors meet their housing needs, tend to fall short of providing adequate health and nutritional support. The retirement-facility industry has responded to this with *low-income housing*, a need-based style of living that now houses about 10 percent of American seniors.

LA POSADA AT PARK CENTRE, GREEN VALLEY, ARIZONA

Each patient room has plaid bedspreads and custom casegoods. Artwork is conspicuously and intentionally absent, since most residents prefer to bring their own, thereby personalizing the space. (Architecture: Englebrecht and Griffin; interiors: Life Designs; custom casegoods: Caseworks, Inc.; bedspreads: Cohama; flooring: Armstrong; seating: Thonet; photo: Ed Rosenberger.)

MAYFLOWER RETIREMENT COMMUNITY, WINTER PARK, FLORIDA

LEFT: Residents at the Mayflower furnish their own apartments, with finishes and fixtures selected as part of the rental package. Here the screened-in porch has been converted to a sun room. (Architecture: Fugleberg Koch Architects, Inc.; interiors: Design Collective, Inc., in association with Spaces Inc.; photo: Philip Eschbach.)

SURREY PLACE,
CHESTERFIELD, MISSOURI
—————————————————
Brass lamps, prints, and bleached
oak furnishings make the resident
rooms cozy. Vertical louvers are
used at the windows because
they catch less dust than horizontal
blinds. (Architecture: The
Wischmeyer Architects; interiors:
LVK Associates; bed: Huntco;
casegoods: Kimball; lamp:
Prestige; valence, bedspread:
Lazarus Contract; chair: Kimball
with fabric by Atlanta Architectural
Textiles; artwork: MBL; wall
border: Satinesque Sophisticates;
photo: Alise O'Brien.)

The benefits of low-income housing for the seniors segment go beyond shelter and include independence, medical assistance, and nutritional requirements. Effective low-income seniors housing is designed to supply life's basic needs, but seldom does it provide for an individual's personal wants. And indeed, going beyond the minimum level of housing necessary for decent living is rarely the intent—individual spaces within a low-income housing development are small, usually the size of a studio apartment, but adequate, and are sometimes shared. While this housing is spartan, many low-income seniors find these facilities to be superior to the accommodations they endured as children or middle-aged adults.

Low-income housing usually does not offer a wide range of diversity in step-down care. The assumption is that residents are ambulatory, and any care for nonambulatory individuals is relegated to government-assisted programs in private nursing facilities or government-owned long-term care facilities.

On the other end of the spectrum, roughly 65 percent of the seniors market now lives in private housing facilities marketed to upper-middle- and upper-income consumers. Seventy percent of newly constructed seniors facilities are affordable only by these two income levels. The majority of these facilities, constructed and completed in the late 1980s and early 1990s, offer a broad range of social, recreational, educational, and medical programs, as well as sophisticated campus designs offering a broad range of physical amenities. Independence and convenience are maximized by offering these options on an à la carte basis. The development of these facilities is largely market-, preference-, or demand-driven.

The 1990s bring a great need for alternative offerings that are available and affordable to middle-income seniors. The demand for this type of housing will continue to increase as the parents of the baby-boomer generation move toward old age and the need for congregate housing and care. This is probably the ripest area of development for the retirement housing industry today—the majority of the seniors population, 65 percent, fits within this middle-income group, and models for middle-income housing have largely been ignored. Wise developers will take note and plan accordingly.

UNIT SIZE AND DESIGN. During the 1970s, the trend was toward small congregate living units, usually from 650 square feet (60 square meters) for one bedroom to 1,200 square feet (112 square meters) for two bedrooms. This seemed desirable from a facility's economic point of view, but developers soon discovered that living-unit size was the single most negative factor perceived by the market. Most residents were not pleased with moving from their present 2,500- to 4,000-square-foot (232- to 372-square-meter) homes to much smaller homes or apartments, even though the smaller units were more manageable. Moving to the small apartments generally meant disposing of or storing furnishings and valuables, which many residents understandably found troubling.

Furthermore, many potential residents are not emotionally prepared to deal with the prospect of moving into smaller quarters and into a new phase of life, thinking, "I'm not old yet. I'm not ready for this." While this negative impression of small space can be overcome by skillful design, the current trend is simply toward larger living units (often three-bedroom, two-bath units), which also generate higher rents. Most congregate living units today range from 750 to 1,800 square feet (70 to 167 square meters), with the average unit size in the vicinity of 1,200 square feet (112 square meters).

Fortunately, most potential residents do not perceive the multifunctional use of public and private space within a congregate living setting as a negative. For example, living room/dining room areas or bedroom/den/crafts areas are often shared as single rooms, following a national housing trend toward the concept of a "great room" that may serve a number of uses, such as dining, informal gathering, meal preparation, entertainment, arts and crafts, and study, with satellite rooms for bathing and sleeping.

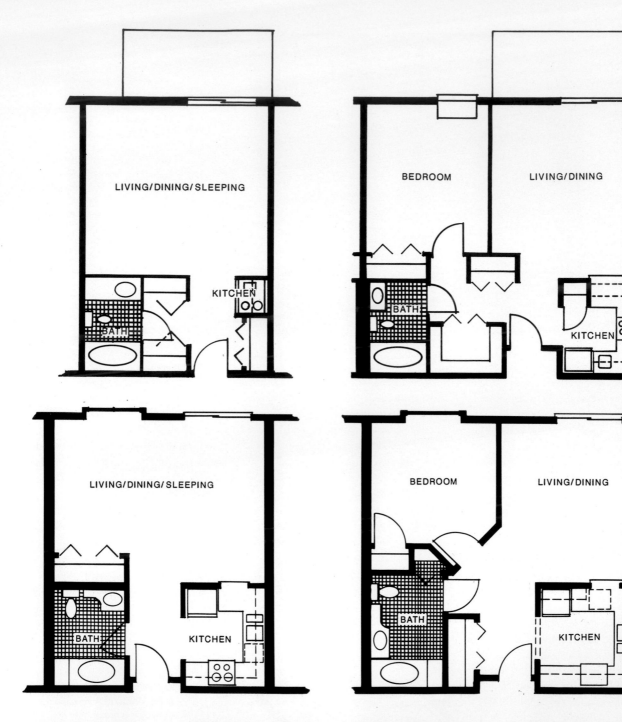

TYPICAL EFFICIENCY UNIT—1970s

TOP LEFT: This type of unit was generally accepted for congregate living during the 1970s. Approximate total area: 300 square feet (28 square meters). (Illustration: Douglas Smith/Life Designs.)

TYPICAL ONE-BEDROOM UNIT—1970s

TOP RIGHT: This configuration was fairly typical of its type in the 1970s. Approximate total area: 500 square feet (47 square meters). (Illustration: Douglas Smith/Life Designs.)

TYPICAL EFFICIENCY UNIT—1980s

BOTTOM LEFT: Note the more generously appointed kitchen, as well as the increase in dimensions for all function areas, in comparison with the 1970s efficiency example. Approximate total area: 425 square feet (40 square meters). (Illustration: Douglas Smith/Life Designs.)

TYPICAL ONE-BEDROOM UNIT—1980s

BOTTOM RIGHT: As with the efficiency unit, this 1980s one-bedroom example represents an improvement over its 1970s counterpart. Approximate total area: 575 square feet (53 square meters). (Illustration: Douglas Smith/Life Designs.)

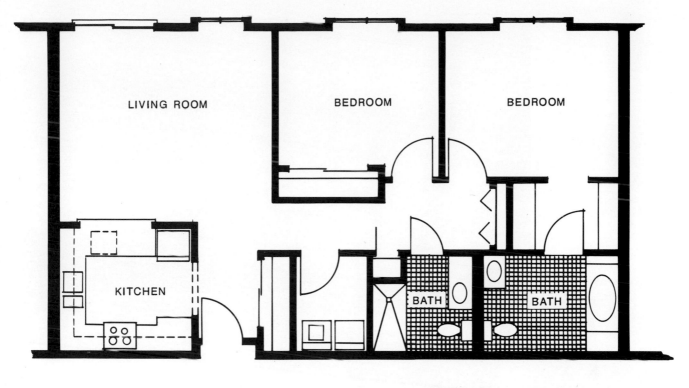

LIVING ROOM

BEDROOM

BEDROOM

KITCHEN

BATH

BATH

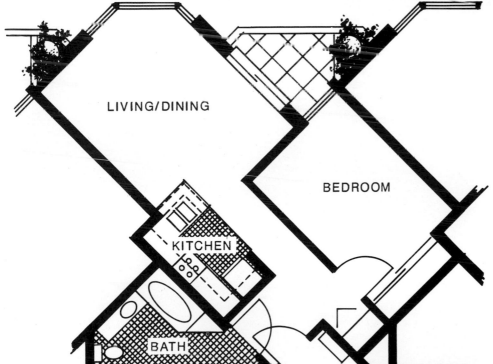

LIVING/DINING

KITCHEN

BEDROOM

BATH

TYPICAL TWO-BEDROOM UNIT—1990s

ABOVE: Demand for two-bedroom units has increased in the 1990s, driven by residents' desires to move from larger homes to apartment housing without having to sacrifice most of their furnishings and possessions. Approximate total area: 1,000 square feet (93 square meters). (Illustration: Douglas Smith/Life Designs.)

TYPICAL ONE-BEDROOM UNIT—1990s

LEFT: An innovative and functional use of space has been coupled here with a reasonable sense of cost-efficiency. This creative yet practical combination is likely to continue in the 1990s, as rising construction costs play a greater role in project feasibility. Approximate total area: 475 square feet (44 square meters). (Illustration: Douglas Smith/Life Designs.)

THE RENAISSANCE, AUSTIN, TEXAS

ABOVE: The white columns, horizontal banding, and arched entryways used on the exterior of The Renaissance help to "tie the nine buildings together," says architect David Farrell. (Architecture: Good Fulton & Farrell; interiors: ABV & Associates; photo: Peter Paige.)

LEFT: The site plan shows the U-shaped configuration of the buildings, with the commons building in the top center. The building at the bottom of the plan is the Anna Hiss House, the original residence on this former ranch property, now used as a second amenity building and as guest quarters. (Architecture: Good Fulton & Farrell.)

Some major corporations are buying into this concept to the point of investing millions of research and development dollars in products to further this concept of multifunctional space. The trend is also evidenced in other ways: Formerly, fixed structural walls were the norm for the division of space according to programming and usage, but now the tendency is to provide minimal interior walls. Freestanding dividers functionally and creatively divide space without isolating the space from other areas, thus allowing for an abundance of functions.

An increasingly popular concept among middle-income seniors who are single, is that of a shared, detached dwelling unit—also called *shared housing*. Each unit will generally have four to six single-occupancy bedrooms (sometimes single-gender, sometimes coed), each connecting to a single-occupancy bathroom. The bedrooms are all satellites to a great room, where a variety of other functions can take place, including dining, gathering, meal preparation, entertainment, and so on. Sometimes the floor plan includes additional rooms, such as a formal living room, den, or activities room. Within this concept of living, each resident participates in shared tasks of daily living, such as cooking, housekeeping, shopping, bill paying,

COTTAGE PARK PLACE,
SACRAMENTO, CALIFORNIA

The assisted living residences are grouped into clusters of 13 living units, each cluster with its own activity/dining room and lounge area. Each living united is located a short distance for its cluster's common areas. (Architecture: Irwin Architecture Partnership.)

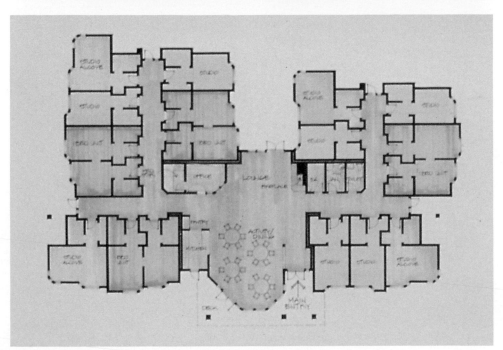

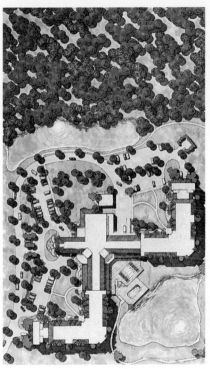

yard maintenance, trash removal, and transportation, which are usually rotated among the residents. This trend may constitute a genuine revival of the communal living arrangements that were popular among today's middle-aged adults when they were younger, in the 1960s.

A surprising number of benefits have been found from this model of living, led by cost-effectiveness for those on limited incomes. Secondary benefits include companionship, social and emotional sharing, and a sense of feeling needed and useful within the unit. This arrangement also fosters independence while maintaining a real sense of community within a mini-neighborhood or a quasifamily setting. In short, these settings provide a dignified life-style within a semiprivate setting.

CAMPUS TYPES. Nothing affects the functional ability of a campus more than its physical layout. A number of approaches are possible.

Low-rise construction, while less costly than multiple-story, high-rise construction, squanders land and creates problems of sheer distance that staff and residents must travel (usually by foot) to get around the campus. High-rise construction, on the other hand, presents problems in terms of structural and mechanical systems, costs, service centralization, and residents' inherently less intimate relationship with the surrounding site. In inner-city areas, vertical design is usually the only option.

The trend in the 1980s was toward suburban campuses of 20 to 60 acres (8 to 24 hectares). Campuses of this type have a broad range of offerings including detached dwelling units or cottages, congregate apartment units, and assisted living and skilled nursing facilities all on the same campus. Most of the buildings are one to four stories high. Many campus layouts are designed in an A, X, H, or cruciform plan, with centralized common amenities available to all residents, usually in the form of a clubhouse or commons building. Covered walkways allow residents to traverse the campus, but many of these large campuses are structured in a way that forces a resident to travel several times per day for such simple services as meals, mail, and social activities, with distances as lengthy as one city block in each direction.

THE BREAKERS AT GOLF MILL, DES PLAINES, ILLINOIS

ABOVE: The building's A-shaped footprint allowed the architects to position most of the commons spaces just a few steps away from the central atrium. (Architecture: The Loewenberg/Fitch Partnership.)

LEFT: A focal table with an oversized floral arrangement gives the reception area the look of a luxury hotel. (Architecture: The Loewenberg/Fitch Partnership; interiors: Design 1 Interiors; table: Pietro Studios Custom Glass; rug: Masland; tile: Villeroy & Boch; wallcovering: Vycon; vase: Sylvestri; photo: Jamie Padgett, Karant & Associates.)

RIGHT: In the main dining area, the designers strove to maintain a uniform level of brightness without glare. A contemporary flame-stitch patterned fabric adds interest to the sturdy armchairs, which are easy to rise from. (Architecture: The Loewenberg/Fitch Partnership; interiors: Design 1 Interiors; chairs: Shelby Williams; fabrics: Kravet Fabrics, American Contract Technology, Duralee Fabrics; carpet: Durkan; lighting Fixture: Originals 22; wallcovering: Norton Blumenthal; pottery: Niles Accessories; china: Dudson; silverware: World Tableware International; photo: Jamie Padgett, Karant & Associates.)

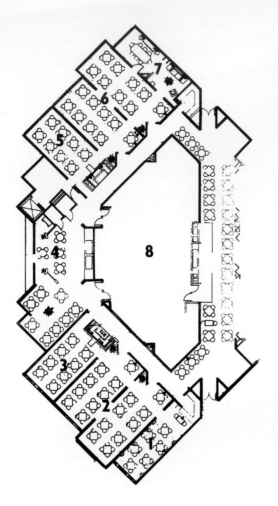

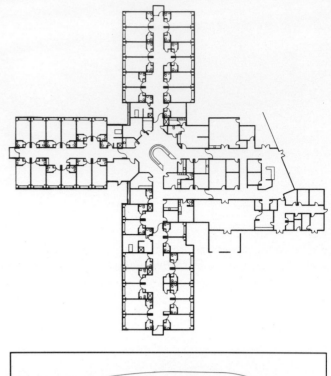

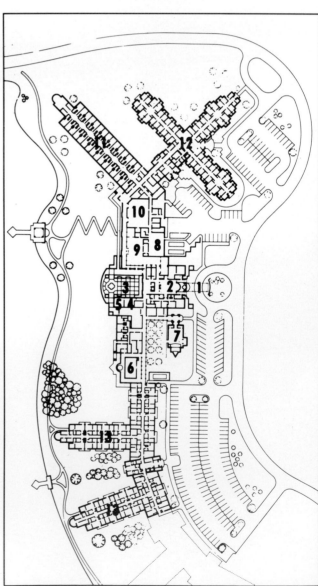

FREEDOM PLAZA, SUN CITY, ARIZONA

ABOVE: A floor plan of the sixth level shows dining and lounge areas encircling the kitchen. Legend: 1. Williamsburg Room (private dining). 2. Traditional Room. 3. Spanish Room. 4. Lounge and overflow dining. 5. English Traditional Room. 6. Arizona Room. 7. Art Deco Room. 8. Kitchen. (Architecture: Freedom Group Inc.)

LA POSADA AT PARK CENTRE, GREEN VALLEY, ARIZONA

TOP RIGHT: This floor plan shows the facility's cruciform layout. (Architecture: Englebrecht.)

ST. CATHERINE'S VILLAGE, MADISON, MISSISSIPPI

Site plan legend: 1. Porte-cochere. 2. Lobby. 3. Courtyard. 4. Deli. 5. General store. 6. Natatorium. 7. Chapel. 8. Kitchen. 9. Independent dining room. 10. Assisted living dining room. 11. Assisted living wing. 12. Skilled nursing wing. 13. Independent apartment wings. (Architecture: Cooke Douglass Farr, Ltd.)

There is some concern that these common campuses may become liabilities as residents age. As one developer has commented, "We do not want to be in the busing business for simple services, such as meal service, as residents get older." Indeed, one facility has had to resort to specially designed golf carts to serve food in individual residential units. With these concerns in mind, the current trend is toward more compact building layout (even though many campuses may retain expansive grounds, often with walking paths included for those who want to walk greater distances), with basic services and destination points located closer to the residential living units.

Although the H and X plans have been popular for many congregate housing developments for reasons of centralizing common amenities, design deficiencies often exist at the outer extremes of many projects laid out in this manner. For example, the apartment wings are often located along extremely lengthy runs of corridors, with numbered portals identifying the apartment entrances. These long corridors, often poorly or incorrectly lit, often look so shabby that one wonders if the money ran out, or if everything was budgeted for the facility entrance, lobby, and dining space.

New architectural and design trends are toward smaller campuses and residential clusters with fewer apartment units and shorter runs of corridors. Instead of employing repetitive, monotonous corridors with an endless series of doorways, an effort is being made to group apartment units in clusters of six or eight, much like small neighborhoods, with congregating areas in expanded corridors. Many designs cluster residential units with small dining, living, and recreating space, with services (especially food) brought to the cluster and enjoyed in this shared space. This reduces the operational costs of delivering room service to each residential unit and offers a more intimate dining experience than a 300-seat central dining room in a commons or clubhouse building. Moreover, clusters can be segregated by care level (independent living, assisted living, or skilled nursing) or separated into specialty clusters designed for Alzheimer's residents and similar groups with specialized needs regarding care, supervision, and medical attention.

BROOKHAVEN AT LEXINGTON, LEXINGTON, MASSACHUSETTS

Leather-upholstered wingback chairs, dark woods, and brass accessories create a restful, traditional mood in the library. Clerestories and full-length windows allow light indoors. (Architecture: Russell Gibson von Dohlen; interiors: Arthur Shuster, Inc.; carpet: Charleston Carpets; chairs and fabric: Drexel Heritage; desk: Hooker Furniture; casegoods: Drexel Heritage; lamp: Frederick Cooper; fireplace accessories: Gatco; artwork: painting by David Laakso through J. Todd Galleries; photo: A. F. Payne Photographic.)

FORWOOD MANOR, WILMINGTON, DELAWARE

ABOVE: An Oriental rug chosen for the lobby area is well-anchored to minimize the risk of spills. (Architecture: Moeckel Carbonell Associates; interiors: Interior Design Associates; photo: Tom Crane.)

RIGHT: Window valances ensure that natural light from the courtyard across the corridor will reach the dining area. The blue-gray vinyl wallcovering is easy to care for and imparts an upscale look. (Architecture: Moeckel Carbonell Associates; interiors: Interior Design Associates; chairs: Chairmaster with P. Kaufmann fabric; tables: L&B Contract Industries; buffet: Wellington Hall; carpet: Lees Commercial Carpet; draperies: P. Kaufmann, fabricated by Fantagraph; photo: Tom Crane.)

THE PARKLANE, A CLASSIC RESIDENCE BY HYATT, MONTEREY, CALIFORNIA

Rows of books line the walls of the cozy library, where recessed lighting and a low ceiling help to create a feeling of intimacy. (Architecture: Mogens Mogensen, AIA; interiors: Design Corner, Inc.; photo: Milroy/McAleer.)

CAMPUS PERSONALIZATION. A strong and healthy trend is the personalization of the campuses for individual residents. In facilities from the 1970s and 1980s, residents were frequently overheard commenting, "It's a lovely place, but it's not home." The designer's task is to create opportunities for residents to develop a sense of the familiar, a sense of making their own mark within their own personal territory. This type of design, which gives the residents a sense of control over their environment, applies not only to personal space but to common spaces as well.

To help achieve this, planners and designers need to create flexible multifunctional spaces that can accommodate a broad range of activities. Resident committees or focus groups with prospective residents can reveal a wealth of information on what the residents want and will use in such spaces. Display and showcase areas, community information boards, closed-circuit television with retirement community messages, newsletters, lecture areas, craft and workshop areas, open spaces for physical activities, reference areas, computer facilities and equipment, and demonstration areas are among the offerings that can allow senior residents to help control and personalize their surroundings.

Many campuses now show evidence of the facility having been altered to meet the specific needs of various resident interest groups. Other campuses are designed with open space for later development based on community interests. On many campuses, the residents are in control of social, recreational, and educational program agendas. All of these are examples of letting the residents create their own space, thereby making the facility their home. The costs of these approaches are usually negligible when compared to the long-term gain in terms of marketing, sales, and word of mouth.

Designers and planners should remember that many seniors "retire" only from their business careers—in their social, recreational, and avocational interests, they maintain full agendas. Indeed, many seniors see themselves as finally having an opportunity to catch up on these nonbusiness affairs after devoting their earlier years to work, family, and so forth. Retirement facility developers, planners, and designers should keep all of this in mind when plotting out prospective facilities—the results can be rewarding for the facilities and their residents alike.

REFERENCES

Dychtwald, K., and Flower, J. 1989. *Age Wave*. Los Angeles: Jeremy P. Tarcher, Inc.
Erickson, J. 1988. *Wisdom and the Senses*. New York: W. W. Norton.
Spence, A. 1988. *Biology of Human Aging*. Englewood Cliffs, N.J.: Prentice-Hall.
Ward, A. 1984. *The Aging Experience*. New York: Harper and Row.
Wolfe, D. 1990. *Serving the Ageless Market*. New York: McGraw Hill.

SUGGESTED READINGS

Atchley, R. 1971. Retirement and Leisure Participation: Continuity or Crisis. *The Gerontologist*. November: 13–17.
Cumming, E., and Henry, W. 1961. *Growing Old*. New York: Basic Books.
Roman, P., and Taietz. 1967. Organizational Structure and Disagreement: The Emeritus Professor. *The Gerontologist*. July: 147–52.

CHAPTER EIGHT

FINANCING

THE GATESWORTH
AT ONE McKNIGHT PLACE,
ST. LOUIS, MISSOURI

In the lobby, as in the other public spaces, the dominant colors are purple, rose, teal, and peach, a palette that flattens most skin tones and remains attractive to the aging eye. (Architecture: Arthur J. Sitzwold & Associates; interiors: LVK Associates; seating, tables: Hickory Business Furniture with upholstery fabric by Architex; carpet: Jack Lenor Larsen; lighting: Gross Chandelier; wallcovering: Carnegie Xorel, Schumacker & Co.; wood floor: Permagrain; ceiling: Armstrong; marble tile: Marble Technics; etched glass: custom made by Art Glass Unlimited; artwork: Joan Hall, B. Z. Wagman Galleries; photo: Barbara Eliott Martin.)

One of the most significant challenges facing the developer or owner of a senior living facility is finding capital to finance the project. Tax issues must also be considered, since the effect will be realized at the bottom line.

Capital (or sources thereof) can be broken down into two basic forms—debt and equity—with an extensive range of options available within each of these two groupings.

DEBT FINANCING

Simply stated, debt financing options obligate the developer or owner to pay back debt borrowed from lenders. The debt may be partially secured by a contribution from the owner in the form of a down payment. Under a debt-financing arrangement, the owner holds title to the property while the lending institution has a lien against the title, which means the owner cannot sell the property without the consent of the lending institution (which would certainly necessitate satisfying the debt). With the passage of the 1986 Tax Reform Act, which created tougher syndication tax rules, longer depreciation schedules, higher minimum tax rates, lower marginal tax rates, and limitations on deductions of investment interest, the once-formidable incentives toward traditional debt financing have all but disappeared.

Incentives or no, however, debt financing continues to be used. Debt financing methods include mortgage financing (zero-coupon, participating, traditional, and securitized), bond financing (taxable, high-yield, or "junk," and tax-exempt), coinsured debt (including Housing and Urban Development and Federal Housing Administration mortgage insurance), bank borrowing, and credit enhancements.

Bank borrowing from commercial banks is a primary source for construction financing, primarily because it is quick and requires little up-front money. Construction loans are generally provided for a maximum of two to three years, with higher interest rates than those charged to working-capital loans and fixed-asset loans. Most banks require a "takeout" from an insurance company or mortgage banking firm—a commitment from a large lender who agrees to assume the debt from the commercial bank at the completion of the project's construction.

Banks generally have not made long-term commitments for retirement community development, primarily because they do not understand the industry or the related services and medical care that go along with it. As a result, the best way to secure a bank loan is to know the banker personally.

Banks (especially thrifts or Savings and Loans) have been hard hit by bad real estate loans in the commercial office building markets. This will make the early and middle 1990s difficult times for obtaining conventional bank financing. But as McGovern (1988) points out, "The bank loan . . . has two major deficiencies: (1) the term of the loan will usually not exceed 10 years and (2) the interest rate will be a variable rate at some level at or above the prime rate." Since most retirement facility projects are financed for longer than 10 years, this may result in very high borrowing costs during refinancing, and since the prime rate has varied from 4 to 24 percent, profitability calculations can be difficult, if not impossible, to determine. A new product banks are offering is the interest rate cap, essentially a form of insurance in which the borrower can pay the lender a fee to cap its interest rate at a certain level.

For large projects, developers may seek foreign investment from overseas banks, which may have easier borrowing restrictions. Japanese investors are interested in the United States real estate market because of the favorable exchange rate from yen to dollar, and they recognize the political and economic stability offered by American markets.

Conventional *mortgage financing* continues to be a major option for retirement centers, and is one of the quickest methods of financing. Conventional mortgages "lack the restrictions often contained in government financing programs such as an inclusionary requirement, the prohibition of an entrance fee, or maintenance of a large reserve fund" (Gimmy and Boehm 1988). To be sure, conventional mortgages have higher cost factors than government-supported financing, and a developer must weigh these additional costs against the reduced time frame from project inception to completion. Calculating when a project will begin its cash flow will influence the developer's decision in this regard.

Life insurance companies and pension funds are the major sources of mortgage funding for real estate projects. Mortgage bankers are becoming more familiar with the retirement product, learning that senior living facilities are combinations of housing, services, and limited medical care. In addition to these factors, lenders are aware of the long absorption rates for senior facilities, and they therefore require evidence of adequate working capital and sufficient cash reserves before approving loans. If the organization planning to operate the facility cannot demonstrate a successful track record, lenders may consult one of the several management consulting firms specializing in various aspects of senior housing. These firms' specialties include feasibility, marketing, leasing and sales, operations (i.e., housekeeping, maintenance, and foodservice), and so on. Moreover, lenders may require an appraisal before granting the loan. Most mortgage bankers will finance only 75 percent of the cost of a senior living facility which suggests that the developer/ owner must provide 25 percent of the financing through equity sources (Gimmy and Boehm 1988).

A *securitized mortgage* is a security (something that is given, deposited, or pledged in order to make certain the fulfillment of an obligation) backed by a first mortgage on certain real property. The mortgage security is divided into certificates, each of which represents an undivided interest in the first mortgage note, and the borrower sells mortgage certificates to lenders to mortgage the property.

While securitized mortgages offer flexibility—the borrower can offer the lenders bonds that mature at different times (securing a lower blended yield) or can offer a zero-coupon bond with no interest or principal due until maturity (Kneen and Kelly 1987)—there are high costs involved in preparing to offer the securitized mortgage.

A *zero-coupon mortgage financing package* permits the borrowers to pay neither interest nor principal on the loan until maturity, when the balance for both principal and interest is due. The advantages of this approach are significant: During the first few years of development and operation, which are typically lean cash-flow years, the facility is not responsible for principal payments to retire the debt, or even for the debt service, allowing the property to achieve a steady cash flow sooner, which is attractive to investors and to the developer/owner. On the other hand, the accumulation of debt can negate any accumulation in the equity or appreciation, leaving no equity remaining in the property at maturity because the compounded interest and the principal have eaten into the equity. With this in mind, the zero-coupon debt should not exceed two-thirds of the original acquisition cost of the retirement community (Roche 1987).

A *graduated-payment* or *negative-amortization mortgage* offers some characteristics of both the zero-coupon mortgage and the conventional mortgage structure. In this type of mortgage, only a portion of the interest due is payable during the first few years of the loan, with the remaining interest added to the unpaid principal balance. As the project fills and begins to cash flow, principal and interest payments increase to an appropriate level to retire the debt for the duration of the amortization period.

In a *participation mortgage*, lenders offer attractive loan rates in return for a percentage share of both the cash flow and the capital gain or appreciation upon sale of the facility, making the lender a partner of sorts. The borrower should "expect to pay a couple of points over prime, 15 to 20 percent of appreciation on the building and two points in origination fees" (Roche 1987). This participation mortgage structure has been in existence for years, and the size of the market is much larger than one might expect. Borrowers should approach lenders with this type of structure.

Public credit enhancements, coinsured debt or *mortgage insurance* through the federal department of Housing and Urban Development (HUD) through its Federal Housing Administration (FHA) provide the only federal insurance for congregate housing. Mortgage loans insured by the FHA are typically sold to one or two investors or packaged into mortgage securities guaranteed by the Government National Mortgage Association (GNMA, or *Ginnie Mae*). The Federal National Mortgage Association (FNMA, or *Fannie Mae*) and the Federal Home Loan Mortgage Corporation will provide debt financing in terms ranging from five to fifteen years for refinancing existing projects. Of particular interest is that in early 1989 Fannie Mae announced a nationwide $100 million project to buy mortgages designed specifically for seniors.

Under Section 221(d)4 of the 1983 National Housing Act, HUD formed Retirement Service Centers (RSCs) to fund congregate housing. "Facilities under this new program would be limited to market rate, elderly tenants, would exclude direct medical care, and would likely provide a meals, services, and amenities package which exceeds any normally submitted under [the old] Section 221(d)(4) program" (HUD 1983). In June of 1988, the 155 projects in the RSC pipeline averaged 148 units each and a mortgage amount of $57,231 per unit, according to HUD (Shashaty 1988).

While many developers have sought government insurance as their preferred financing method, the HUD/FHA insurance can be so high that it would be foolish to use it for financing a low- to

moderate-income project (McGovern 1989). HUD and FHA provide long-term bond insurance that guarantees a "AAA" rating from Standard and Poors or Moody's Investor Service, but it should be made clear that HUD and FHA do not issue the debt, but *insure* the debt, which is the guarantee required to attract investor capital. When employed appropriately, the advantages of HUD/FHA insurance include nonrecourse basis (i.e., the lender cannot hold the borrower personally liable for the real estate loan), a 10-percent ceiling on the developer's contribution to the project's cost, and the guarantee of a fixed annual interest cost for 40 years (McGovern 1989).

Funding is also available via Section 223(f). Under the FHA Section 223(f) coinsurance program, an eligible property is any existing rental housing property of more than five units that is more than three years old, and mortgaged properties currently held in a coinsurer's

portfolio that have not been in default or modification for at least two years—provided that loans from the lender's portfolio cannot exceed 25 percent of the lender's coinsured loans in any 12-month period. 223(f) renovation limits are that cost of repairs cannot exceed the greater of 15 percent of the property's value after repair or $6,500 per dwelling unit plus equipment, and no more than one major building component may be replaced.

Private credit enhancements, which include letters of credit (LOCs) that a lending institution prepares for client, bond insurance, or guarantees, are means of converting low-quality financing into high-quality financing through the use of a third-party guarantee. They are issued primarily because the borrower cannot attain a good credit rating on his or her own merits. The procedure generally is as follows: A letter of credit is issued by a bank, insurance company, or savings and loan company certifying that the lending

CLASSIC RESIDENCE
BY HYATT,
TEANECK, NEW JERSEY

Stainless steel, modern mauve chairs, and gold-framed mirrors mark the club room as a departure from the Classic Residence's otherwise traditional ambience. (Architecture: Fusco, Shaffer & Pappas, Inc.; interiors: Culpepper, McAuliffe and Meaders, Inc.; carpet: Floorgraphix; custom millwork: Confab; bar stools: Shelby Williams; seating: Kisabeth; fabric: Unika Vaev, Brunschwig & Fils; tables: Appleton; porcelain: China Sea Trader; photo: Gabriel Benzur.)

CLASSIC RESIDENCE
BY HYATT,
TEANECK, NEW JERSEY

The private dining room seats
eight for formal dinners.
(Architecture: Fusco, Shaffer &
Pappas, Inc.; interiors: Culpepper,
McAuliffe and Meaders, Inc.;
carpet: Trafford Park Carpets.
Dining chairs: Hospitality Furniture
Company; fabric: AAT, Fonthill;
casegoods: Thomasville;
chandelier: Alger Lighting; art:
Fine Art, Ltd.; china: Lenox;
flatware: Oneida; napery: Artex;
glassware: Cardinal; photo:
Gabriel Benzur.)

institution will insure the debt against default if the borrower cannot make principal and interest payments. Bonds then carry the rating of the lending institution (typically "AA" or "AAA"), rather than the borrower's rating. Bond insurance guarantees the payment of both principal and interest in case of default, and, as with LOCs, carries the bond rating of the insurer. Bond insurance, however, may be difficult to obtain, due to various restrictions and the developer's track record. Most LOCs will cost between 0.5 and 1 percent per year, and a collateralized letter of credit will increase the cost to between 1.5 and 2 percent (McGovern 1988).

Bond financing may include tax-exempt bonds, taxable bonds, and high-yield or "junk" bonds. Tax-exempt bond financing has been popular for retirement communities, and there are certain tax benefits to this approach. To qualify, the housing units must contain separate and complete facilities for living, sleeping, eating, cooking, and sanitation—in short, there must be a living room, bedroom, kitchen, and private bath. Moreover, this type of financing is not available for transient housing, such as hotels or nursing homes.

Because of their nontaxable status, the interest rate on tax-exempt bonds averages from 2 to 2.5 percentage points below taxable market rates. Furthermore, tax-exempt bonds allow for a flexible loan period, varying from five to forty years and can offer 100 percent financing at these long-term fixed rates. In addition, the credibility derived from the bonds' tax-exempt status can be used as a marketing device.

There is, however, a cost associated with the lower interest rate obtainable on tax-exempt bonds: the need to satisfy numerous governmental restrictions. The process takes longer than conventional financing, and up-front costs are higher, as well, including those for the banker, bond counsel, depository trust company, issuer, loan origination points, underwriter's discount and counsel, surety, trustee, rating agency, and bond printing (Mortgage Banker's Association 1990; Gimmy and Boehm 1988).

Taxable bonds or market-rate bonds, are similar to tax-exempt bonds but are more quickly processed, are negotiated at less cost, and are not restricted by the IRS regulations that govern tax-exempt bonds. The several disadvantages of taxable bonds include a higher interest rate that must be paid as well as up-front issuing costs. The maturity term for taxable bonds is usually shorter than for tax-exempt bonds, and taxable bond interest rates reflect the current state of the bond market. Taxable bonds tend to mature in 10 to 15 years with 20- to 25-year amortization schedules, but there are two ways the maturity can be lengthened through negotiation of a private placement with a 20- or 25-year maturity or creation of an obligation with a 20-year maturity where the interest rate is adjusted on an indexed basis every five to ten years (Kneen and Kelly 1987).

Even for taxable capital financing, there is an advantage in having a state authority issue the bonds. If the bonds are publicly issued, however, the sponsor must obtain letters of credit or bond insurance to obtain the best possible rating and, therefore, a lower interest rate.

High-yield income bonds or junk bonds are highly speculative bond issues for the investor. For the developer, the costs under this method will be less than with a conventional loan from a traditional lender, and the interest rate or debt service will be fixed rather than variable, but the risks are high. During the 1980s, junk bonds were used to finance corporate takeovers, mergers and acquisitions, and leveraged buyouts, but the scandals of Drexel Burnham Lambert and Michael Millken have cooled the junk bond market.

In essence, high-yield bonds are unrated debt, and any number of smaller, regional brokerage companies, some insurance companies, and assets managers may be able to arrange for private-placement debt. Private-placement front-end costs are usually lower than

public-placement costs, but the interest rate paid for privately placed debt is higher than for public debt. In addition, there is less need for public disclosure than with public placements. "Expect to pay a spread of four percentage points over the . . . yield on 30-year Treasury bonds and two to four points in origination/sales fees to the agent who places your debt" (Roche 1987).

EQUITY FINANCING

Equity financing differs from debt financing because the developer/owner's ownership interest is diluted by selling some or all of his or her ownership in the property. This ownership allows the equity capital holders to have a claim on both income and assets of the company secondary to the claims of the creditors or of those who hold the company's debt. Depending upon the form of ownership, those holding equity may be able to share management or operational responsibility for the property. Equity "partners" usually share in both the downside risk and the upside potential in the project; those holding debt usually do not share in the upside potential and are paid an agreed-upon amount (interest plus principal) in the case of a shortfall in revenues over expenses. While there is a shortage of available debt financing, leading to equity financing's increasing popularity, "distinctions between debt and equity blur as an increasing number of lenders take a participation in projects they finance, and as equity partners demand guaranteed returns" (Mortgage Banker's Association 1990). Equity financing methods include developer financing, syndications, limited partnerships, real estate investment trusts (REITs), joint ventures with either national or local sponsors, venture capital, and resident financing through deposits or fees.

A *developer/owner's own assets* may be used to fund a project. These assets may be land that the developer already owns, cash that the developer is willing to commit to the project, or construction labor and/or materials that the developer is willing to dedicate to the project. A developer may also pledge to provide the

ongoing management (termed "sweat" equity) once the facility is operational in return for a percentage ownership share.

Syndication or *limited partnership* is a financing option that is expensive to create and sometimes cumbersome to operate. A syndication is a group of persons or concerns who combine to carry out particular transactions; a limited partnership is comprised of one or more general partners, responsible for the total financial well-being, management, and implementation of a stated business purpose, and limited partners, who are financially responsible only for a stated, limited amount of capital and are *not* permitted to manage or operate the concern. "Publicly offered partnerships must be registered with the Securities and Exchange Commission and often involve front-end fees of 20 to 30 percent of the money raised. Private partnerships are less complex, but can be marketed only to investors who meet minimum net worth and income requirements" (Mortgage Banker's Association 1990). Yet several major syndicators have expressed interest in retirement housing, making more capital available to developers and owners. Indeed, syndicators may become potential owners, thereby increasing the value of successful projects. Even with the restrictions of the Tax Reform Act of 1986, syndications continue to generate tax losses and income growth for investors, making investments in retirement living facilities attractive possibilities. In order to encourage investors, high cash returns and guaranteed rates of return are being offered.

A *real estate investment trust* (REIT) is an association, corporation, or trust (something held by one party for the benefit of another) in which the trustees of the organization own and hold title to real estate assets or invest funds in real estate ventures. REITs that take an equity interest are becoming popular capital sources for retirement facility development, particularly as opposed to those that only make mortgage loans.

A *joint venture* is "an association of persons jointly undertaking some commercial enterprise. It requires a community of interest in the performance of the subject matter, a right to direct and govern the policy in connection therewith,

Two dining rooms accommodate large groups—one is contemporary, the other traditional. The Traditional Room, shown here, features upholstered valences, cane-back chairs, and bold floral carpet. (Architecture: Freedom Group Inc.; interiors: Merlino Interior Design Associates; chairs: Hickory Furniture; tables: The Chair Factory; wallcovering: Lappin; carpet: Durkan Patterned Carpet; ceiling: Armstrong; lighting: Boyd Lighting, Winona; window treatment: Dazian's Inc.; photo: James Cowlin.)

and duty, which may be altered by agreement, to share both in profit and losses. . . . A one-time grouping of two or more persons in a business undertaking. Unlike a partnership, a joint venture does not entail a continuing relationship among the parties" (Gerber and Feinstein 1985). The organizational form of the venture (e.g., partnership, corporation, and so on) is less important than the compatibility of the partners.

Joint ventures in the development of retirement housing includes affiliation with both national and local sponsors. Affiliations with national sponsors might include a local developer joining forces with a national company developing senior living housing (e.g., Forum Retirement Partners, Marriott Senior Living Division, Classic Residences by Hyatt, and so forth), with insurance companies, or with other national financial institutions.

On the other hand, a developer may look for a local health care provider with local market identity, minimizing risk while simultaneously seeking long-term

capital appreciation; in a well-matched situation, a local not-for-profit institution may have excess capacity and need to diversify its operations while looking for development expertise and financial backing. A joint venture undertaken by a private developer and a not-for-profit institution, like a hospital, may be particularly advantageous if the not-for-profit organization has land with easy zoning-approval potential on which to build. Agreements between such parties need to specify clearly who will do what, and when, who gets the profits, and in what proportion, and who is responsible for losses, and in what proportion.

Venture capital firms have begun to express interest in investing in retirement housing. Venture capitalists provide equity capital to retirement living projects and usually require either a significant ownership interest for their capital contribution or substantial collateral. They seek business opportunities with tremendous upside potential and understand that their business is, by nature, high-risk. Indeed, most venture capital firms are satisfied with one success in 20 investment attempts. Historically, they invest in biomedical products, high technology, and specialized manufacturing products, tending not to invest in services, property development activities, or operational ventures. Their long-term interest in retirement housing is suspect, primarily due to the industry's protracted payback and traditional rates of return when compared to high technology and biomedical products and research.

Another financing method, and a quite popular one, is using the capital provided by the present or future *residents*, usually in the form of entrance or endowment fees. It is worth noting that these have come under heavy regulation because of abuses by providers. While some of these transgressions were not necessarily unethical—they resulted from either bad management or the tendency of retirement facility residents to outlive the actuarial tables—the increased regulatory environment has slowed down the development processes when initial endowment or entrance fees are used as the sole basis for development capital. As supplements to a larger financing package, however, such fees offer flexibility to the developer.

Residents can also be a funding source if the developer chooses to use a condominium or cooperative structure. Under such a scheme, the developer presells the condominium or cooperative before it is constructed and uses the resulting funds to finance development. Alfred Holbrook (1987) writes that because of the limited access to other forms of equity financing, this approach will soon become the most prominent form. Indeed, the tax advantages for the buyer make this arrangement beneficial to both developer and resident. Developers should note that while the cooperative structure can be used in conjunction with federal housing subsidy programs, condominiums cannot be conjoined with HUD or FHA programs.

REFERENCES

Gerber, L., and Feinstein, F. 1985. Key Issues in Establishing a Joint Venture—An Agenda for Discussion. Presentation for the National Real Estate Development Center.

Gimmy, A., and Boehm, M. 1988. *Elderly Housing A Guide to Appraisal, Market Analysis, Development and Financing.* Chicago: American Institute of Real Estate Appraisers.

Holbrook, A. 1987. Development of Senior Adult Housing Using Equity Financing. *Contemporary Long-Term Care.* April: 35–39.

Kneen, W., and Kelly, N. 1987. Discovering Alternatives for Financing Senior Housing. *Healthcare Financial Management.* November: 65.

McGovern, G. 1988. Financing Assisted Living Projects Through the Private Financial Markets. *Retirement Housing Report.* October.

———. 1989. Is HUD Bond Insurance Appropriate for Your Retirement Housing Project? Unpublished paper.

Mortgage Banker's Association of America. 1990. Chapter Five—Financing Alternatives for Multifamily Retirement Housing. In *Strategies for Senior Housing Underwriting.* Chicago: Probus Publishing Company.

Roche, R. 1987. Debt Financing and Senior Living Facilities. *Contemporary Long-Term Care.* June: 38–40.

Shashaty, A. 1988. Retirement Service Centers Face Marketing Obstacles, Size Limits. *Senior Living News.* September: 13.

SUGGESTED READING

Habighorst, A., and Hirschfield, J. 1987. Sources of Financing for Congregate Housing. *Mortgage Banking.* July: 10–14.

CHAPTER NINE

MEDICAL AND LONG-TERM CARE INSURANCE

ST. CATHERINE'S VILLAGE,
MADISON, MISSISSIPPI

Appointments in the Skylight dining room revitalize classic forms, but "with no connection to any one period," says Dorothy King, a member of the interior design project team. The rear doors lead to one of two private dining areas. (Architecture and interiors: Cooke Douglass Farr, Ltd.; carpet: Durkan Patterned Carpet, Shaw Industries; wallcovering: Essex; paint: Benjamin Moore; chairs: Hickory Business Furniture with F. Schumacher fabric; tables: Falcon; photo: John O'Hagan.)

The understanding and study of Medicare and Medicare supplemental insurance (Medigap) policies is critical for any administrator of a retirement facility. Knowledge of Medicare's reimbursement features will also assist in a facility's marketing efforts, especially for the assisted living and skilled nursing components. For those who have not worked in this area, the complex medical insurance environment can be confusing to say the least, so it is important to distinguish between Medicare, Medicaid, and Medigap.

Medicare is a federal program, instituted in 1965, that generally covers any person who reaches the age of 65 (certain disabled individuals under 65 are also eligible). Qualified Medicare beneficiaries have *premium-free* Medicare hospital insurance benefits (Part A) based upon their own or their spouse's employment. Those under 65 can qualify for Medicare hospital insurance (Part A and Part B) if they have been on Social Security or Railroad Retirement disability for more than 24 months. A person 65 or older who, for whatever reason, does not qualify for Medicare can purchase Medicare by paying a monthly premium at an annually determined rate.

Other terms that must be understood include the following: *Hospital insurance* (Part A) is designed to cover inpatient hospital care, some inpatient care in a skilled nursing facility, and some health and hospice care; *medical insurance* (Part B) covers doctor's services, outpatient hospital services, durable medical equipment (walkers, wheelchairs, and so forth), and other medical supplies and services not covered by hospital insurance; *coinsurance* is the term used to describe the sharing of expenses between the patient and the insurance company, under which Medicare pays 80 percent of the cost of the covered health service and the patient pays the remaining 20 percent.

Medicare does not cover private-duty nursing or most nursing home care costs (except after a three-day stay in a hospital), but there are other medical insurance policies that may be purchased to supplement Medicare. These include: Medicare Supplement Insurance (Medigap), nursing home or long-term care insurance, membership in a health maintenance organization (HMO), and employer or association group insurance.

Medigap is a generic term used to describe supplemental insurance to Medicare. Actually, the term is a misnomer because *gap* implies that there is some type of publicly funded coverage available beyond Medicare, but such is not the case. Medigap or supplemental insurance is any voluntary, contributory private insurance plan available to Medicare beneficiaries to cover the costs of medical, health, and physician's services not covered by Medicare.

**NEWPORT BAY
CONDOMINIUMS,
INDIANAPOLIS, INDIANA**

Palladian fan light windows, a
columned entryway, and a
widow's walk balustrade at the
peak of the roof lend Early
American character to the facility's
facade. (Architecture: Wolner
Associates; interiors: Eden Design
Associates; photo: Dan Francis,
Mardan Photography.)

Medicaid is a program administered
by the individual states and funded by
both the federal and state governments
on a shared basis. Medicaid makes payments for approved health services provided by hospitals, health agencies, and
other medical service providers for welfare recipients or those whose income
does not exceed the maximum welfare
benefit.

TYPES OF INSURANCE
CARRIERS

No discussion of medical insurance
would be complete without defining the
various types of insurance carriers in the
medical field. In short, an insurance carrier is an underwriter of risk. The importance of understanding insurance for a
retirement operator is imperative. Should

the facility have an SNF, intermediate
care (ICF)/assisted living (ALF) component, home health, or similar medical
service provider, partial payment for
these medical services might very well
come from various insurance carriers.

Perhaps the most widely known and
understood carrier is Blue Cross/Blue
Shield, a nationwide federation of local,
not-for-profit community service organizations who contract with physicians and
other health-care providers to provide
payment for medical and other health-
care services to their policyholders or
subscribers. Among insurance professionals, this type of insurance is referred
to as an *indemnity plan*, or *wraparound*.
Many other insurance carriers, including
UNUM, Aetna, Prudential, Amex Life
Assurance, John Hancock, The Hart-
ford, Liberty Mutual, and so forth, also
have extensive medical insurance

programs similar to Blue Cross/Blue Shield's, as do various reinsurance companies, such as General Reinsurance, Employer's Reinsurance, Cologne Reinsurance, American Reinsurance, Continental Reinsurance, and so forth. Traditionally, reinsurance companies would serve as insurance wholesalers, underwriting the primary insurance carriers' portfolios; now, reinsurance companies are offering their services directly to retirement centers who chose to self-insure.

Indemnity plan carriers offer their policyholders or subscribers unlimited choices of physicians and health-care providers for medical services. Under these plans the insurance subscriber purchases a plan authorizing a certain level of benefits to be covered, agreed upon by the carrier, the physician, other health-care providers, and any other parties involved. The health-care providers are paid (either by the insurance company or by the patient, who in turn is reimbursed by the insurance company) on a fee-for-services basis and charge prevailing market rates. In general, indemnity plans cover expenses for acute medical services and do not cover preventive work (e.g., annual physicals).

Outside the retirement center setting, indemnity plans do not usually provide for ALF or ILU living facilities unless certain medical services, such as diagnostic medical equipment, walkers, wheelchairs, and so forth, are provided. Medicare Part A benefits would generally not be covered in an ALF or ILU.

If a retirement organization contracts with an indemnity plan carrier, it usually provides a *long-term care policy* with the medical insurance package. A long-term care insurance policy is designed to guard against catastrophic costs of long-term care, and provides comprehensive coverage for home health care, adult day care, respite care, and nursing home stays for all care levels (skilled, intermediate, and custodial) with no prior institutional stay required. The resident, if enrolled through a group in the retirement center setting, can pay for the premium as a charge added onto the monthly statement, or the retirement home may bundle this fee with other fees, particularly if membership in the medical plan is compulsory.

Independent practice associations (IPAs) are regional organizations that enter into contracts with specific health-care providers to deliver services at agreed-upon rates with agreed-upon conditions (e.g., a 90-day filing limit). Health-care providers with independent contracts with the IPA are not IPA employees—rather, they are listed as "in-network" providers to IPA subscribers, who receive improved benefits coverage by using these network providers. Membership in an IPA offers the advantage of local management of healthcare quality and cost. Moreover, IPAs will cover urgent or emergency care, whether from an in-network provider or not, at whatever rate it is billed (indeed, IPAs are usually successful at holding nonmember providers to the Medicare rate for Medicare-covered patients).

Health Maintenance Organizations (HMOs) contract with physicians, (called *Primary Care Physicians*, or PCPs), hospitals, and long-term care and other health-care providers to deliver health-care services to their subscribers. With a few exceptions, referrals to contract and noncontract health-care providers must be made by the patient's primary care physician, and a subscriber must use one of the HMO's designated health-care providers and be referred to specialists by the primary care physician or else neither the HMO nor Medicare will pay for the services. Preventive care is covered, and in many cases is actually encouraged.

HMOs assume the medical payment risk for their subscribers. Medicare no longer reimburses the subscriber or the health-care provider, as the HMO assumes all administrative responsibilities. Medicare does, however, pay the HMO a per-member, per-month rate (referred to as a *capitated rate*) for the HMO's provision of Medicare services. HMOs cover all fees for covered Medicare services, plus some additional benefits, but they may charge Medicare subscribers an additional premium (in 1990, one HMO charged $55 per month) for each of its Medicare subscribers.

HMO Medicare beneficiaries can be enrolled through a group (e.g., a retirement center), but each individual in the group has his or her own plan or policy with the HMO, meaning that families and spouses cannot be "joined" with a family member or spouse. The retirement center resident may pay for the premium as a charge added onto the monthly statement, or the retirement home may bundle this fee with other fees. (The *staff model HMO*, a variation of the HMO, is an organizational entity that employs a staff of physicians or other health-care providers who have certain centralized locations within a service area. Otherwise, the same benefits and limitations that describe a traditional HMO are consistent with the Staff Model HMO.)

A *preferred provider organization* (PPO) is an insurance company that contracts with certain providers of medical services who offer a cost savings for subscribers, as well as for the insurance carrier, if the subscriber uses a designated preferred provider. If a subscriber chooses to use a medical service that is not a preferred provider, the member must pay a higher fee, but the member retains this choice and is reimbursed for a portion of the expense. As with indemnity plans, PPOs usually do not provide for ALF or ILU living facilities unless certain Part B medical services are required and needed.

Each of these models may be coupled with benefits for prescription medications, although reimbursement for subscription medications may become problematic for SNF or ICF residents, whose medications are administered by a nurse from the facility's own supply inventory.

LONG-TERM CARE INSURANCE

Medicare nursing home benefits provided by Medicare are very modest, and should not be considered effective for most retirement centers. As described previously, many facilities supplement their packages by offering long-term care insurance, a relatively new product for private insurance companies that was introduced in the 1970s in response to elderly consumers' fears that nursing home costs could wipe out their life savings, destroy their independence, and land them on welfare. Recently, insurance companies have been marketing the long-term care product directly to retirement communities, a development to the benefit of retirement communities, as the increase in market competition among insurance carriers has led to a wide variety of insurance plan design options.

One of the more difficult aspects of long-term care profitability for the insurance industry, and an acute problem for the individual retirement community, is the *spread of risk*. For the most part, the people who recognize the need for long-term care coverage and are able to pay for it are in the highest risk category—their very ability to see the necessity for having such coverage is likely to mean they will soon be in a position to fall back upon it. With this in mind, it will be necessary to focus future sales and marketing efforts of the long-term care product on groups outside the middle-aged consumers who currently seek out the product. Unless this can be achieved, the distribution of risk will never be sufficiently widespread to make the coverage profitable.

While long-term care insurance has not performed particularly well for the insurance industry, many carriers are nonetheless committed to the product and are giving it every chance to become profitable—clearly, demand for the product is heavy. The numerous factors that need to be resolved for both subscribers and the insurance companies include, but are not limited to, guaranteed renewal; a marketable maximum term (e.g., two years, five years, lifetime); a marketable daily deductible amount; adjustments for inflation; coverage for different care levels, including comprehensive coverage; marketable provisions for Parkinson's, Alzheimer's, and other senility diseases; preconditions (or lack thereof) based on prior hospitalization or prior nursing home residency; and age-based premium increases.

The long-term care insurance options offered with retirement community residency differ from generic long-term care policies. This is due in part to the *home health inclusion*, an insurance provision that provides insurance coverage for services delivered in a patient's private residence, which substitutes for more expensive and sometimes unnecessary institutional care. This provision, touted as keeping residents in their ILUs and thereby lowering costs, may have negative consequences for the retirement facility. For instance, keeping a resident in his or her ILU may pose difficulties when management needs to fill an empty unit with a new resident, since prospective residents who see themselves as healthy, independent, and not truly "old" may not warm to the prospect of living next door to someone who requires frequent or constant medical attention.

Most long-term care insurance policies include a *waiver of premium* feature, which, as the name suggests, allows the insured party to maintain coverage and continue receiving benefits without paying a premium in the event of income interruption or similar financial difficulties. While this feature is sensible for policyholders with full-time jobs, who would find paying the premium a financial hardship during a period of recovery, it is inappropriate for retirement home residents on fixed incomes, who tend not to be *earning* income. Despite this, many retirement communities that add long-term care insurance to their packages insist that the premium waiver provision be included by the insurance carrier, believing it to be an essential marketing tool needed to compete effectively with rival facilities.

Is all the fuss over premium waiver worth the effort? Although many retirement communities go to great lengths to obtain the premium waiver feature, one insurance industry figure feels their efforts may be misdirected (MacKenzie 1990):

Many retirement communities continue to request the premium waiver feature because of a perceived need to compete with individual insurance policies. However, is a retirement community competing against a long-term care insurance policy or is the community competing against

alternate life styles? To the extent that the retirement community emphasizes the availability of long-term care insurance, the community is either not sure of, or has missed, their market.

In fact, successful retirement communities attract prospective residents because of the total atmosphere and service package of the community, not one component of the program. Moreover, an emphasis on long-term care insurance over the total attributes of living in the retirement community will attract an older and more frail clientele. In the insurance industry this is known as adverse selection. These people, as a group, will tend to use more services, generate more claims, leading to premium increases that, while predictable, are nevertheless painful . . .

Indeed, because of adverse selection in the retirement community market, at least one large insurance carrier has canceled its retirement community policies. It is worth noting that some of this carrier's retirement community clients were experiencing significant marketing problems and added long-term care insurance as a way to "improve" their residential product.

The *couple purchase option* should be considered to be an exception to the premium waiver feature. When two people living in the same residential unit have a dependent relationship, this feature effectively protects them from undue, excessive financial exposure. If both members of the couple are in an ALF or SNF, this provision should be offered, but only as an option, so that single residents are not forced to subsidize all residents (as would be the case if the waiver of premium were instituted to all couples across the board).

In terms of long-term care insurance, everyone involved should keep in mind that *rate guarantees* are only as good as the risk pool generating the premium payments. Level-premium programs anticipate that claims against the long-term care policy will be negligible in the first few years, and that the additional revenue generated will be able to be drawn down against in subsequent years. If the actual utilization of the long-term care insurance exceeds these projections, residents may experience substantial increases in their premiums, despite initial claims to the contrary. The insurance industry refers to this, aptly, as a "phantom benefit."

Clearly, when designing long-term care insurance products, both insurance carriers and retirement centers (especially if they are the sum-total of the risk pool) must use caution in offering features that may not be necessary and may cause severe financial problems for both. Just as care and caution are necessary during the original development and feasibility of a retirement community, similar attention needs to be paid to the development of each of the benefits it offers.

REFERENCES

MacKenzie, R. 1990. Long Term Care Insurance: Plan Design Options for Retirement Communities. Unpublished paper. March: 1–8.

SUGGESTED READINGS

Diamond, L. 1989. Rental Units with a Long-Term Care Benefit: A Potential Marketing Niche. *Retirement Housing Report*. February: 2–3.

Greenberg, J. 1989. Long-Term Care Insurance for the 1990's. *Spectrum*. July/August: 12–15.

Kunerth, A. 1987. Group LTC Insurance as a Marketing Tool. *Contemporary Long-Term Care*. December: 38, 108–24.

———. 1989. Integrating Long-Term Care Insurance in the Marketing Programs of Senior Living Communities. *Retirement Housing Report*. October: 7–10.

INDEX